RESILIENCE
NAVIGATING CHALLENGES
IN MODERN LIFE

Fielding University Press is an imprint of Fielding Graduate University.
Its objective is to advance the research and scholarship of Fielding faculty, students and alumni around the world, using a variety of publishing platforms.

For more information, please contact Fielding University Press, attn. Dr. Jean-Pierre Isbouts, via email to jisbouts@fielding.edu, or via postal mail to Fielding Graduate University, 2020 De la Vina Street, Santa Barbara, CA 93105. On the web: www. fielding.edu/universitypress.

Library of Congress Cataloging-in-Publication data
Resilience in a Complicated World
1. Social Sciences – Social Psychology

RESILIENCE
NAVIGATING CHALLENGES
IN MODERN LIFE

Edited by
Marie Sonnet, PhD
Fellow, Institute for Social Innovation, Fielding Graduate University
Connie Corley, PhD
Professor, Fielding Graduate University

TABLE OF CONTENTS

INTRODUCTION

In everyday discourse, being "resilient" has become a common adjective. In popular and academic literature, increasing "resilience" is promoted as a desirable goal for individuals, organizations, communities, and even our planet. Being ubiquitous, however, brings risks of meaninglessness and rote adoption with insignificant impact. Practice can be marked by a rush to simplicity and a loss of profound complexity. To be effective in studying and building resilience, scholars, educators, and practitioners need to experience deeper understanding and engage with more evidence across a range of applications. These are the goals of this volume of the Fielding Graduate University Monograph Series, *RESILIENCE: Navigating Challenges of Modern Life.*

Applying resilience in practice calls for sorting out what is meant by resilience in real circumstances – detailing what it means, how it is observed and assessed, where it is applied, if or why it offers value, and how it can be strengthened. To this end, we present six articles by ten authors who use original academic research to analyze and discuss core aspects of resilience in practice, deepening our understanding of a profound and promising human attribute and promoting more research for evidence-based applications not only for individuals, but for families, organizations and our communities.

Our authors explore the adaptation and growth experience of social actors within the boundaries of particular ecosystems and problems – cultural, socio-economic, geographic, organizational, political, and communal. They offer the scholar, educator, and practitioner a scan of how the properties of resilient people and systems work, increasing our awareness of the complexity and variety of the resilience concept. For example, we learn that disruption and resilience move in long-term cycles of action and feedback, eluding the quick fix, and that resilience can also be a property of human systems that are not of good intent. The strategies presented by our authors reflect such complexity, creating value for the reader.

Zieva Dauber Konvisser, *Resilience and Vulnerability in Aging Holocaust Survivors and Their Descendants,* describes resilience across generations in response to searing involvement in the Holocaust. Rebecca Stafford and Andrea Meier, *Trajectories of Resilience for Whistleblower Psychological Trauma,* discuss the resilience and recovery of trauma experienced by whistleblowers, noting that roughly 50 to 60 percent of people in the U.S. are exposed to some kind of significant, traumatizing stressor in their lifetimes. Trisha Gentle, *Voices of Women: Oppression and Resilience,* examines the resilience of women who have experienced abuse and oppression. Marie Sonnet, *Employee-Built Organizational Resilience Capacity: Getting to Specific Beliefs and Behaviors,* explores organizational resilience capacity as a strategic asset built by employees as they work together. Pearl L. Seidman, *Ecotones: How Intersectional Differences Spur Adaptation and Resilience,* details the experience of cultural connectors who foster resilience "at the edges" of a Korean American community in a Maryland county. Finally, Connie Corley, David Blake Willis, Diyana Dobberteen, and Eliza von Baeyer, *Cruzando Puentes / Crossing Bridges: Building Resilience Through Communitas,* describe how older adults and former gang members are building bridges to community resilience through a story sharing process. We are very grateful to our authors. They generously offered their work to deepen and broaden the efforts of others seeking to understand and apply resilience scholarship.

Resilience is most often presented as a positive characteristic. Indeed, our authors discuss resilience as both a valuable capacity to be fostered in preparation for change and adversity and as an activated capability for growth in complex and even dire circumstances. The dynamics of resilience vary from work that is done individually (Gentle; Stafford & Meier), in families (Konvisser), in organizations (Sonnet), and in communities (Corley, Willis, Dobberteen, & von Baeyer; Seidman).

One paradox of resilience is that it is most visible amid tension, turbulence, and trauma. Another is that growth is the result of adversity. This is evident as our authors discuss resilience as both an adaptive and transformative characteristic. Sonnet notes that tension is inherent in a process that requires organizations to both retain identifying characteristics and to self-reorganize for renewal and invention. Indeed, as Seidman observes in her study of cultural intersections in Howard County, Maryland: "Without tension there is no reason to adapt or build adaptive potential. Tension was a trigger for individual and collective elasticity—in behavior, ways of seeing, social networks, and innovation." Acknowledging that growth depends on friction invokes viewing resilient human systems as complex, adaptive, socio-ecological systems.

Evidence for this approach appears in the circumstances and tensions that accompany activated resilience. These tensions reveal that resilience also resides in persistent accompanying forces and entities, some of which are negative and even evil, including ongoing illegal behavior in a public sector organization (Stafford & Meier), a clash of gang culture and gentrification (Corley et al.), prejudice that resists immigrant inclusion (Seidman), the scourge of Nazi death camps that seeps into generations (Konvisser), abusive behavior towards women (Gentle), and relentless change complicated by surprise and adversity that challenge organizations and their communities (Sonnet).

All provoke a profound human response. Konvisser summarizes that response in this way: "While they do not forget their traumatic experiences, many survivors are able to integrate and own the painful emotions of their situation, make them part of their story, and live with them in a productive way." There is enormous power in such a response.

Indeed, resilience is a remarkable capacity. Our authors maintain that resilience capacity can be deliberately accessed, strengthened, and even transmitted. One strategy is the power of storytelling. In a classic use of research as "giving voice to", authors Gentle, Seidman, and Stafford and Meier use the words of participants to situate their experiences and demonstrate the mechanisms of resilience-building. Corley et al. and Konvisser show the power of passing stories of resilience along to others. Sonnet includes telling stories of times we solved problems together in her set of group-based behaviors in a resilient organization.

An important understanding emerges. While resilience implies recovery and anticipates a new, stronger state, it does not follow a tidy N-step process. Stafford and Meier show how personal trauma changes the brain and they discuss specific trauma-informed therapies that demonstrate promise for healing brain and body and achieving post-traumatic growth. They maintain that "resilience efforts were not single events, but a long-term developmental process." Corley et al. describe a social transformation process using a community of practice approach. Gentle, Seidman, and Konvisser demonstrate how growth may be generational, as experiences of both adversity and recovery are woven into families and communities. Sonnet maintains that organizational routines, practices, norms, and inducements create a communal climate that either supports or deters collective resilience. Resilience, then, is a long-term characteristic of complex systems built to last.

Perseverance is a core attribute of a resilient system. Our authors consciously observed their own perseverance over the course of preparing their articles. It was surprising to track the challenges each person faced and how often the characteristics of a resilient response were required. Health crises, family deaths and births, political turbulence, natural disaster, job difficulties, and the pressures of elder care presented unexpected challenges that required what Sonnet calls "a storehouse of capabilities." Themes of *grace under pressure* and *everyday strength* prevailed. We are most grateful to all.

But our work shows that resilience in practice is more than that. Gentle observes in her study of oppressed women: "There was a consistent surfacing of coping, understanding, adaptation, and even healing that demonstrates resilience." Corley et al. find in Los Angeles that "...the yearnings and struggles of diasporic communities commemorate historical memory, power, and resistance that have cultural identity at the core of the changes we witness over time – reflections of ethnicity, race, and gender in particular eras." Konvisser concludes, "While each experience is unique, by bringing forth and understanding some of the common qualities and sources of strength that help people cope with the tragedy and uncertainty and survive the long-term impacts of extreme prolonged trauma, we provide valuable insights and evidence for the traumatized individuals themselves; for their families, friends, and communities supporting their recovery."

It is our hope that this collected work provides scholars and practitioners more evidence to understand and successfully impact the resilience of individuals, families, organizations, and communities. As Seidman notes, access to diverse resources allows us to "exceed the bounds" of what we understand and what we can imagine. Our future depends on it.

We are deeply grateful for the additional reviewers who guided the authors (in last-name alphabetical order): John Austin, PhD, Barton Buechner, PhD, Anna DiStefano, PhD, Tracy Fisher, PhD,

Zieva Konvisser, PhD and David Blake Willis, PhD. The leadership of Fielding President Katrina Rogers and the vision of Dr. Jean-Pierre Isbouts to mobilize the Fielding Monograph series and books published by Fielding University Press have made our contribution to scholarship and practice possible.

Marie Sonnet, PhD, Co-Editor   Connie Corley, PhD, Co-Editor
Pittsburgh, Pennsylvania   LosAngeles, California

CHAPTER 1:

RESILIENCE AND VULNERABILITY IN AGING HOLOCAUST SURVIVORS AND THEIR DESCENDANTS

Zieva Dauber Konvisser, PhD
Fellow, Institute for Social Innovation, Fielding Graduate University
Adjunct Assistant Professor of Criminal Justice, Wayne State University

Abstract

This chapter discusses what we know about resilience and vulnerability in Holocaust Survivors and their descendants and their ability to move alongside, and even transcend, the trauma and to age successfully. It provides an overview of the human impact of trauma, in general, and of the Holocaust, in particular, in both Adult and Child Survivors, including the protective factors and coping strategies that have enabled positive outcomes, the risk factors that increase vulnerability, the aging process itself which may add complications for some Survivors and their families, and the manifold ways of finding meaning and purpose through the struggle with trauma. It also describes what we know about the transmission of both trauma and strength to family members of Holocaust Survivors. Furthermore, it addresses the lessons we can learn from this to improve the lives of other victims of the Holocaust and similar atrocities.

Keywords: Holocaust, trauma, Survivor, posttraumatic stress (PTS), resilience, vulnerability, recovery, posttraumatic growth (PTG), personal strength, transcendence, aging, meaning, purpose, Second Generation, Third Generation, trauma transmission

Introduction

Over the years, much has been written in the popular press about the trauma experienced by Holocaust Survivors, about the transmission of trauma to their family members, and about the aging process itself, which may add complications for some survivors and their families. Historically there has been an overemphasis on their problems, yet many Survivors and their descendants are high functioning, have adapted to the long-term impacts of their traumatic experiences, demonstrate resilience, and have been able to create families and lead productive lives paradoxically alongside of persisting negative sequelae of trauma.

The chapter begins with a discussion of the human impact of traumatic events, in general, and the potential responses to trauma, ranging from posttraumatic stress to resilience and posttraumatic growth, and how these may coexist. The focus then shifts to the impact of genocidal trauma on survivors of the Holocaust – both Adult and Child Survivors, the protective and risk factors for resilience and vulnerability, the impact of the aging process on Survivors, their manifold ways of finding meaning and purpose in their struggle with life's most challenging circumstances, and the consequences for their descendants. In closing, it addresses the lessons we can learn from Holocaust Survivors and their descendants to improve the lives of other victims of the Holocaust and similar atrocities.

The Human Impact of Trauma

Traumatic events can overwhelm the ordinary systems of care that give people a sense of control, connection, and meaning; overwhelm the ordinary human adaptations to life, and shatter our fundamental assumptions about ourselves and our world. Thus, trauma results in feelings of intense fear, helplessness, loss of control, and threat of annihilation and inspires helplessness and terror. In addition, trauma produces profound and lasting changes in our ability to feel, think, and do (Herman, 1997). However, the frightening and confusing aftermath of trauma also may be fertile ground for unexpected outcomes: "While survivors of trauma have learned that the world is evil and meaningless, that life is terminal and that people are unworthy, they have also experienced that there may be hope even in the worst of their experiences" (Janoff-Bulman, 1992, p. 169).

Individuals vary in their responses to trauma, ranging from *succumbing;* to *survival with impairment,* as in posttraumatic stress; to *resilience* or *recovery,* bouncing back to the pre-adversity level of functioning after experiencing hardship, trauma, or adversity and moving on with life as usual; and to *thriving,* as in *posttraumatic growth,* bouncing forward and surpassing what was present before the event (Carver, 1998).

The American Psychological Association defines *resilience* as "the process of adapting well in the face of adversity, trauma, tragedy, threats or significant sources of stress – such as family and relationship problems, serious health problems or workplace and financial stressors" (American Psychological Association, 2010), while *posttraumatic growth* describes the positive psychological change experienced as a result of the struggle with highly challenging life circumstances (Tedeschi & Calhoun, 2004b; Tedeschi & Calhoun, 1995).

Viktor Frankl, the noted neurologist, psychiatrist, and Holocaust Survivor, describes in his autobiographical *Man's Search for Meaning* (2006), how personal strength, wellness, and other positive outcomes can result from the struggle with a trauma or life crisis and stresses the freedom to *transcend* suffering and the Defiant Power of the Human Spirit to make choices and embrace life.

> ...even when confronted with a hopeless situation,
> when facing a fate that cannot be changed. For what
> then matters is to bear witness to the uniquely human
> potential at its best, which is to transform a personal
> tragedy into a triumph, to turn one's predicament into

a human achievement. When we are no longer able to change a situation... we are challenged to change ourselves. (Frankl, 2006, p. 112)

Trees as Metaphor for Resilience and Growth

Resilience can be conceived as a multidimensional construct that "is evident when individuals are able to resist and recover from stressful situations, or reconfigure their thoughts, beliefs, and behaviors to adjust to ongoing and changing demands" (Lepore & Revenson, 2006, p. 27). A useful analogy is of trees facing strong winds. Some trees may be snapped in half (*distress*), while others remain standing, undisturbed (*resistance*). Trees that bend to accommodate the wind may recover and resume their original upright positions (*recovery* or *homeostasis*). Other trees change shape to accommodate the winds or make the tree resistant to breaking in future wind storms (*reconfiguration*). Some trees may be destroyed, yet still have the capacity to nourish new growth, while others are lifeless (Lepore & Revenson, 2006).

In his book *Aging Well*, George Vaillant (2002) describes resilient individuals as resembling "a twig with a fresh, green living core. When twisted out of shape, such a twig bends, but it does not break; instead, it springs back and continues growing" (p. 285). Trees are also social beings, helping each other through nutrient exchange and in times of need. Like human communities, there are advantages to working together.

On its own, a tree cannot establish a consistent local climate. It is at the mercy of wind and weather. But together, many trees create an ecosystem that moderates extremes of heat and cold, stores a great deal of water, and generates a great deal of humidity. And in this protected environment, trees can live to be very old. (Wohlleben, 2015, pp. 3-4)

Additionally, as they age, "old trees fertilize the forest and help their offspring get a better start in life.... But service in the forest doesn't end when life ends. The rotting cadaver continues to play an important role in the ecosystem for hundreds of years" (Wohlleben, 2015, pp. 65-67).

Who is Resilient?

The manner in which each individual experiences the event, the meaning which each ascribes to the event, and the actions each takes result from his or her personal characteristics, past experiences, present context, and physiological state. Although there is no single factor or magical combination that ensures a positive or negative outcome, certain factors are protective and enhance stress resilience and growth, while others appear to be risk or vulnerability factors for poor adaptation; still others can either support resilience or undermine it depending on their quality or, in some cases, quantity (Butler, Morland, & Leskin, 2006).

Resilience and growth are promoted by the interplay between internal individual factors and external environmental factors. Returning to the tree metaphor, the composition of the tree – soft and pliable like a willow, or hard and rigid like an oak – and the tree's environment – availability of water and nutrients, composition of the soil, or presence of other trees that might buffer the wind or create a protective ecosystem – also significantly impact whether or not it survives to old age (Lepore & Revenson, 2006).

People who are resilient and grow share some common qualities – ones that can be cultivated to master any crisis. These include: positive emotions and optimism, self-confidence, humor, creativity, religion/spirituality, tendencies toward action, altruism, the capacity to recover from negative events, and stress inoculation (Southwick, Vythilingam, & Charney, 2005, 2012; Tedeschi & Calhoun, 1995). In addition, growth is enabled by social support from friends, family, other similarly traumatized people, professionals, society and culture (Calhoun & Tedeschi, 2006), as well as by self-disclosing one's story to supportive others (Tedeschi & Calhoun, 2004b).

Such positive changes can be manifested in several ways. While the encounter with a major life challenge may make us more aware of our vulnerability, it may also change our self-perception, as demonstrated in a greater sense of personal strength and recognition of new possibilities or paths for one's life. At the same time, we may feel a greater connection to other people in general, particularly an increased sense of compassion for other persons who suffer; as a result, we experience warmer, more intimate relationships with others. An altered sense of what is most important is one of the elements of a changed philosophy of life that individuals can experience. A greater appreciation of life and for what we actually have and a changed sense of priorities of the central elements of life are common experiences of persons dealing with crisis. We may also experience changes in the existential, spiritual, or religious realms, reflecting a greater sense of purpose and meaning in life, greater satisfaction, and perhaps clarity with the answers to fundamental existential questions. We may move forward with action as we search for meaning and understanding of the event's significance in our lives (Calhoun & Tedeschi, 2006; Konvisser, 2014).

In the aftermath of trauma, reports of growth experiences far outnumber reports of psychiatric disorders (Quarantelli, 1985; Tedeschi, 1999, as cited in Tedeschi & Calhoun, 2004a). And so, typically, the struggle with the aftermath of trauma can produce a mixture of negative and positive experiences and continuing personal distress and growth often coexist (Joseph & Linley, 2008; Tedeschi & Calhoun, 2004b).

Holocaust Trauma

Genocide in general, and the Holocaust in particular, are and have been acts committed with intent to destroy, in whole or in part, a national, ethnic, racial or religious group. Holocaust trauma is a trauma caused by the Holocaust – the systematic murder of approximately six million Jews by the Nazis in death camps and elsewhere during the second World War. The corresponding Hebrew word is *Shoah,* which means total destruction and refers to the almost complete annihilation of

Jews in Europe by Nazi Germany and its collaborators. Historically, this so-called 'Final Solution' started from the Nürnberg Laws in 1936 and lasted until May 8, 1945 (Kellermann, 2009), although the roots of anti-Semitism go much deeper and back thousands of years. An expanded definition includes Jewish individuals who lived in Europe and were in danger after 1933 with the rise of Hitler because they were in countries controlled by Nazi Germany (Hollander-Goldfein, Isserman, & Goldenberg, 2012).

Thus a *Holocaust Survivor* is broadly defined as any persecuted Jew or other victims who lived under Nazi occupation during the Second World War and who was thus threatened by the policy of the Final Solution but managed to stay alive, including those who were confined to a ghetto, those who experienced forced labor in a work camp and/or incarceration in a concentration camp, those who were in hiding or lived under false identities, refugees who were forced to leave their families behind, those who fought with the partisans (Kellermann, 2009), as well as those individuals who emigrated from Europe prior to the start of World War II (Hollander-Goldfein et al., 2012).

Although there have been other genocides, mass killings, massacres, and traumatic events that may be equally painful and lead to similar posttraumatic stress reactions, and each person's suffering must be acknowledged, in this chapter we are looking principally at Jewish survivors of the Holocaust since this genocide was so much more malignant than many of the other genocides (Kellermann, 2009). And especially for Jews, the Holocaust was unique in its scope and magnitude – the most systematic and effective mass murder in human history, a disaster of enormous proportions perpetrated on a passive civilian population with merciless cruelty and psychological dehumanization (Kellermann, 2009).

What has been reported about Holocaust trauma depends on the questions asked, who the researchers are (e.g., clinicians or researchers), the target population, the nature of sampling (Barel, 2010), and when the questions were asked. In addition, our understanding has evolved in parallel with the major periods of postwar adjustment (Kellermann, 2009).

It began with the terror associated with the Nazi invasion, then the imposition of oppression and practices of discrimination, followed by displacement from home and confiscation of possessions and internment in the ghetto, and, finally, deportation to work or death camps. For some, these events resulted in their escape into hiding and for others in joining resistance units and fighting (Kahana, Harel, & Kahana, 2010).

The immediate aftermath of the Holocaust brought about three challenges for the Survivors. First, Survivors had to come to terms with their own survival; it often took them months to regain some semblance of health. Second, they had to try and find family members who survived and/or come to terms with the losses of most of their family members and friends. Third, they had to try and establish new lives in yet another location which entailed many obstacles and challenges (Kahana et al., 2010).

The 1950s and early 1960s were not only periods of social adjustment and reintegration into society, but also periods of emotional crisis, immigration and absorption, marginalization, and ridicule of those who had not defended themselves sufficiently and had gone like "sheep to the slaughter." Thus, there was a conscious effort not to think too much about the past and to repress traumatic experiences as much as possible (Kellermann, 2009). Furthermore, no one, especially family members, really wanted to hear the Survivors' stories; everyone protected each other from the horrific details of the Holocaust. The resulting "conspiracy of silence" experienced by Survivors in North America when they arrived there shortly after the war, significantly inhibited the healing process (Danieli, 1985). Likewise, until the 1980's in Israel it was not a great honor to be a Holocaust Survivor, and Survivors attempted to be like other Israelis, living through the developmental phase of a Jewish national consciousness.

As a result, initial reports of the psychological impact of the Holocaust were presented mainly by psychiatrists who treated Survivors as patients or by individuals who were applying for restitution funds and had to prove some residual medical or psychiatric disability in order to qualify (David, 2011). These reports focused directly on the Survivors and the atrocities they suffered and their dysfunctions – their "concentration camp syndrome" or "survivor syndrome." Not until 1980 were these symptoms recognized as posttraumatic stress (Hollander-Goldfein et al., 2012).

Following the Eichmann Trial in 1961, the Holocaust became less loaded with social taboo and a more acceptable theme for private and public discourse. The ability to speak was enabled to some extent by Steven Spielberg's founding in 1994 of the USC Shoah Foundation Institute for Visual History and Education, whose mission is to videotape and preserve interviews with Survivors and other witnesses of the Holocaust. Gradually, many individual Survivors started to share their experiences with their families and others as they aged and struggled to resolve repressed memories that may have returned. Beginning in the 2000s, society started to recognize the Survivors' extraordinary accomplishments, giving them final social acceptance and a sense of pride for what they had succeeded to achieve despite everything (Kellermann, 2009).

Because the events were so severe, intense, and long-lasting, the likelihood of developing some kind of posttraumatic stress response after the war was very high, including: chronic posttraumatic stress disorder and its symptoms of repeated nightmares, numbness, and hypervigilance; anxiety, depression and suicide, survivor's guilt, and complicated bereavement and grief (Kellermann, 2009). In addition to the original trauma suffered during the Holocaust, such as powerlessness, fear of annihilation, object loss, and torture (Garwood, 1996, as cited in Kahana et al., 2010), long-term Survivors are also faced with chronic stressors related to the trauma. These include coping with intrusive memories of trauma, living with fear and mistrust, coping with social and psychological isolation, and coping with stigma. Furthermore, Survivors may experience other post-Holocaust trauma, such as the Gulf War Scud missile attacks, as well as having to cope with the normative stressors of aging (Kahana & Kahana, 2001).

In the last two decades, the literature has shifted to a more optimistic focus on posttrauma psychological strength and growth, though still suggesting a divergent picture (Barel, 2010). A team of Israeli and Dutch researchers has analyzed all of the previous research reports involving thousands of Survivors and family members. Their findings suggest that *alongside* the profound and disturbing pain, there is also room for growth (Barel, 2010). Holocaust Survivors exhibit substantially more posttraumatic stress symptoms, but also remarkable resilience (Barel, 2010). Paradoxically, these Survivors may display both vulnerability and resilience, severe traumatization and also extraordinary growth, softness and hardiness, periods of severe suffering and symptomatology, and periods of emotional balance and creativity along with victimization and legacy (Kellermann, 2009).

> *For there is hope for the tree, if it be cut down, that it*
> *will sprout again, and that the tender branch thereof*
> *will not cease* (Job 14:7).

Resilience and Vulnerability in Holocaust Survivors
Like other traumas, how an individual coped with trauma during and after the war is a result of their experiences before, during, and after the war. It is a result of their personality traits, cognitive schemas, and affective experiencing (Hollander-Goldfein et al., 2012) and may vary for each "moment of crisis." Also, like the composition of a tree, protective internal attributions include personal characteristics (e.g., intelligence, skill, the ability to run quickly, hypervigilance, knowledge

and facility with languages, optimism, and lack of fear); will to live or survival instinct; reason to live (following the directives of family members, staying alive to tell the world what happened, desire to reunite with family members, desire for revenge); and agency (making decisions, taking risks, claiming at least partial credit for one's own survival or the survival of others). And like the tree's environment, reported external attributions include the help of others, luck, God, miracle, personal characteristics such as appearance, fate, and random circumstance or pure chance (Hollander-Goldfein et al., 2012).

Trauma also can evoke a wide variety of more or less adaptive coping strategies in Survivors during and after the war, which may lead to psychological well-being. In his 1992 book, *Against All Odds,* Helmreich suggests that there are ten general traits or qualities – protective factors – that were present in those Survivors who were able to lead positive and useful lives after the war. These include flexibility, assertiveness and taking initiative, tenacity, optimism, intelligence or professional skill, distancing ability, group consciousness and belonging to a certain support group, assimilating the knowledge that they survived, finding meaning and a sense of coherence in one's life, and courage.

Greene interviewed Holocaust Survivors to examine protective factors before the war, as well as resilient behaviors during and after the war (Greene, 2002, 2010; Greene & Graham, 2009). The need to survive is a basic human instinct and these Survivors demonstrated the ability to face risks, "exhibiting the self-righting nature of human development" (Greene & Graham, 2009, p. S81). "During and after such critical events, individuals, families, and communities use both their innate and learned abilities (i.e., traits) to engage in actions (i.e., follow adaptive coping strategies) that allow them to respond to the adverse event, deal with feelings of distress, and then to begin to heal" (Greene & Graham 2009, p. S76; Greene, 2010, p. 413). Their responses included a rich array of resilient behaviors: resolving to live, obtaining food and shelter, choosing survival strategies, keeping family ties (trying to save the family), making friends, turning to others and banding together, caring for others, connecting with community, giving testimony, setting up school programs, and writing songs, poems, stories (Greene, 2010).

Holocaust Child Survivors

Child Survivors, defined as those who were less than sixteen years old when the war ended and still under some kind of guardianship (Krell, 2012), were not even recognized as Holocaust Survivors until 1981. They were deprived of their childhood and forced to grow up, literally overnight. They may have been in concentration camps and/or in hiding during the war in private homes, hospitals, orphanages, and convents – sometimes with both parents, with one parent, or with neither parent. Robert Krell, M.D., a Child Survivor and psychiatrist, explains, "We were first generation Holocaust Survivors too young to have advocates for our existence and experiences" (Krell, 2013, p.1).

As a result, "They became little adults with premature responsibilities.... Because a child perceives and remembers things differently than adults, they also cope differently with trauma, forc[ing] them to adapt a variety of different and extraordinary survival strategies that continue all through life" (Kellermann, 2009, pp. 54-55). In addition, since childhood, they have carried the knowledge that they were not meant to exist (David & Pelly, 2003).

In several studies with Holocaust Child Survivors, it was found that the higher their level of personal resources (sense of potency, self-identity, and social support), the less they suffered from posttraumatic stress symptoms and the better their quality of life (Amir & Lev-Wiesel, 2001; Lev-Wiesel & Amir, 2003) and family and marital functioning (Bar-On et al., 1998). In addition to secure attachments with at least one caring adult, there were many other protective factors in varying degrees in these children's lives before the war: various forms of social support, intelligence and social skills, religious belief systems, family values, a developed sense of right and wrong, and stress inoculation from the larger environment of pervasive and brutal anti-Semitism (Hollander-Goldfein et al., 2012).

While their subsequent successful adaptation to life may have contributed to their invisibility, reaching their 50s and 60s has activated the Child Survivors to review their lives and deal with their childhood and traumatic memories by speaking out (Cohen, Brom, & Dasberg, 2001). Through the acts of creation, testimony, and writing, they are able to metabolize the trauma (Feldman, Taieb, & Moro, 2010). While they may suffer more from posttraumatic symptoms, they also may believe that there is justice in the world, that man is in control, that luck exists, and that the world is a good place. This can be understood as a greater need to compensate for the lack of security suffered in childhood by creating a meaningful world in a chaotic reality (Cohen et al., 2001).

Because of the horrendous experiences in their earlier lives, "a sense of rage develops" and many Child Survivors responded not with revenge but with "a desire to seek justice, to teach, and to document the story." As a result, many chose to go into the professions of medicine, psychology, and social work, to "serve as our legacy, a passionate commitment, born of our healing one another, to healing others" (Krell, 2013, p. 2).

Hidden Children

During the time when they were hidden, in addition to being removed from their familiar backgrounds, these children had to remain silent and pretend that whatever life they had before never existed. This was compounded by the trauma of shifting to another identity and separation from their family. After the war, there was the silence of the families. The youngest did not want to hear the stories that the adults had to tell. The adults who had lost children or members of their families in the camps were reluctant to listen to their surviving children's accounts of their experiences (Feldman et al., 2010). As Dr. Krell has written about his experience: "Most of us who were hidden remained hidden. We were the children so comfortable with silence that silence became our vocabulary" (Krell, 1995). Fred Lessing, PhD, a Child Survivor and psychologist, did not speak until 1987; he calls these the "Holocaust-less years" (Personal communication, February 28, 2013).

As a consequence of these experiences, Hidden Children may have presented specific symptoms related to psychological breakdown, to the fact of being Survivors, to the damage to affiliation links, and to losses and impossible mourning. These symptoms were reinforced by silence and by the sometimes-difficult reunions with parents after the war. Children and parents had hoped they would see each other again; idealization on both sides sometimes led to disappointment (Feldman et al., 2010).

Yet, there were protective factors that depended on the child's personality and on the circumstances of his or her life before, during, and after the persecutions. These included: the security of the early relationship, the encounter with a caregiver, a kindly attachment figure who took care of the child and ensured emotional continuity after the parents, protection via siblings, the continuity of care and the continuity of language; nature, the countryside, plants, and animals that acted as resilience tutors; and a reassuring environment, which may have been a community. Supportive coping factors and life choices after the war derived from a dynamic process of affiliations – plans to emigrate to Israel, the search for solutions via psychoanalysis and psychotherapy, or via membership of groups (Feldman et al., 2010).

Such hope also can be symbolized by trees. Anne Frank and her family spent nearly two years in hiding in Amsterdam before being transported to concentration camps and perishing in Bergen-Belsen. While hiding, her exposure to the outside world was limited to what she could see outside her window. "From my favorite spot on the floor,

I look up at the blue sky and the bare chestnut tree, on whose branches little raindrops shine, appear like silver.... When I looked outside right into the depth of Nature and God, then I was happy, really happy" (Frank, February 23, 1944). Watching the chestnut tree cycle through the seasons offered Anne hope that one day humanity also would have another chance. Anne's tree has reached the end of its 150-year lifespan, but it lives on through saplings planted around the world, including one at the Holocaust Memorial Center Zekelman Family Campus in Farmington Hills, Michigan.

Aging Survivors

Many Survivors experience the normal phenomena of old age as a reliving of Holocaust experiences as their children have left home and with the deaths of their spouses and friends. Factors in the histories of some of these families may have created difficulties among parents and children. Older Adult Survivors also tend to dread the inability to work because of deterioration and illness as well as retirement, resulting in loss of structure, routine, self-esteem, status and friends, and the return of memories. They may experience moving or being placed in nursing homes as a recurrence of the disruption in their lives, of being uprooted, dislocated, and incarcerated, especially in the case of hospitalization which may bring about psychotic-like delusions of being in camp again (Danieli, 1994). Survivors who were involved in Nazi medical experimentation during the war may react with fear or mistrust to medical care (David & Pelly, 2003). Furthermore, Survivors remember all too well a world that betrayed their trust in humanity; as they age and must depend on others for care, they must find some way to trust again (David & Pelly, 2003).

As Survivors experience these phenomena, trauma may leave previously resilient Survivors more vulnerable to changes when they are facing stress related to old age, because former coping strategies, such as hard work and taking care of the next generation, are no longer available (Fridman, Bakermans-Kranenburg, Sagi-Schwartz, & van IJzendoorn, 2011). Unwanted unstructured time can reduce defenses and allow room for obtrusive thoughts and other symptoms of posttraumatic stress disorder (David & Pelly, 2003). Traumatic memories and unresolved losses might become more dominant (Fridman et al., 2011), bringing with them both delayed mourning and grief (Kellermann, 2009). The vicissitudes of the normal aging process seem to increase the impact of Holocaust memories and legacies in the Survivors' lives (Isserman, Hollander-Goldfein, & Nechama Horwitz, 2016).

On the other hand, the remarkable resilience that characterized some Holocaust Survivors, in particular in parenting their offspring, could also serve them as they are aging (Fridman et al., 2011). "They may feel surviving into old age is a triumph permitting them to contribute to the maintenance of the culture of a people that was intended to be annihilated" (Kahana et al., 2010, p. 9).

Eva and Boaz Kahana found such a variance in responses in their analysis of 163 narratives of Survivors' assessments of their aging process. Their analysis yielded four major typologies of aging Survivors (Kahana & Kahana, 2001; Kahana et al., 2010). *Resilient agers* express a positive self-concept focusing on sources of strength and a strong sense of values in the face of adversity. *Conditionally vulnerable agers* express a sense of healing from adverse sequelae of the Holocaust with the elapsing of time; however, their wounds are readily opened as they confront new losses or stressors during later life. *Generally vulnerable agers* (also referred to as *premature agers* or *vulnerable aged*) are aging individuals who express enduring distress in the aftermath of trauma; they focus on the overwhelming nature of these negative outcomes and often express beliefs that their traumatic experiences may have precipitated premature aging. *Parallel agers* focus on the comparability of their aging to others who did not endure trauma, feeling that being Survivors of the Holocaust did not make a difference in their experience of aging as a stressor. They may view aging as an equalizer, which metes out normative stressors to all individuals who survive into late life; they may thus view aging as a normalizing influence. Furthermore, "even when elderly Holocaust Survivors show special symptoms of distress, symptomatology may be viewed as normal human psychological reaction to an abnormal situation" (Kahana et al., 2010, p.11).

In the first retrospective population-based cohort study examining age of death among Holocaust Survivors compared to peers without Holocaust backgrounds, against all odds, genocidal Survivors were found to be more likely to live longer (Sagi-Schwartz, Bakermans-Kranenburg, Linn, & van IJzendoorn, 2013). One explanation suggested for this longer life-expectancy is differential mortality during the Holocaust, meaning that those vulnerable to life-threatening conditions had an increased risk to die during the Holocaust, while those who survived were predisposed to reach a relatively old age. An alternative interpretation is that this may be illustrative of posttraumatic growth associated with protective factors in Holocaust Survivors or in their environment after World War II and may highlight the resilience of Survivors of severe trauma, even when they endured psychological, nutritional, and sanitary adversity, often with exposure to contaminating disease without accessibility to health services.

Today the oldest of Child Survivors are in their 90's and the youngest their 70's. Their childhood trauma and how it has affected them differs from the trauma experienced by older Survivors. We are just beginning to learn what will be the impact on the quality of their aging of their early childhood experiences, such as their being separated from parents at critical developmental stages, early parental loss, and forced relocation, their lack of substantial or concrete pre-war memories, starvation, lack of exposure to the outdoors, or the inability to move and wander freely (David & Pelly, 2003). The surviving children of the Holocaust are now older adults and attempting to integrate their horrid life experiences into a semblance of sanity. Studies reported widely in the scientific literature (Barak, 2013) establish the life-long damages caused to Child Survivors of the Holocaust, including severe emotional and psychiatric impairment. As aging adults, they report more dissociative symptoms in everyday life, less satisfaction with their lives, more cognitive impairment, and they also perceive their life events as more stressful as compared to their peers who were not Holocaust Survivors. The Holocaust deprived these Child Survivors of a peaceful legacy.

Moving Alongside and Transcending the Trauma:
Finding Meaning and Purpose

The search for meaning, according to Viktor Frankl is considered to be the primary motivational force in man (Frankl, 2006). Those who are able to find meaning after trauma cope better and are more resilient. While not everyone may find the "why" of their survival, there is strength to be found in the search itself – in the actions taken, by loving another human being, and by the attitude one takes towards unavoidable suffering (Frankl, 2006).

Similarly, a study of how 133 Holocaust Survivors pursued what mattered at three different time points (during the Holocaust, after they immigrated to the United States, and as older adults) found that survival expressed through actions and attitudes was the core theme at all three time points. During the Nazi regime, Survivors kept themselves alive physically by refusing to consider the option of death, being lucky, outwitting the Nazis, stealing, and following a strict philosophy of independence or collectivism. They kept hope alive through believing in liberation, attaching to personal fantasies of what the future might hold, remaining loyal to loved ones, and having faith in their reunion. After immigration, Survivors focused on survival by striving for education and family, having children, being successful, shutting the door to the past, and cultivating proactive attitudes such as gratitude, acceptance, and the dissolving of hatred. As older adults, Survivors' concerns with survival are expressed through maintaining their health, fulfilling their obligations to those who died, and taking principled stands to fight hatred and oppression, "which, in effect, symbolically conveys their defeat of Hitler and the failure of the Final Solution" (Armour, 2010, pp. 440-441).

Thus, many Survivors have found meaning in their own survival during the postwar years. They have rebuilt the Jewish people by starting families of their own, building successful careers, and forming social relationships, as well as supporting and contributing to the survival and building of a homeland in the State of Israel.

Some bear witness and remember the dead by sharing their stories and telling what happened (Hollander-Goldfein et al., 2012; Kahana et al., 2010). Moreover, many, who were previously silent, have come forth to publish their individual or collective memoirs (see Berger, 2001; Epstein, 1979; Clementi, 2013; and Rosensaft, 2015) or record and archive their oral histories through the resources provided by various organizations. These include the USC Shoah Foundation Visual History Archive, the Fortunoff Video Archive for Holocaust Testimonies at Yale, the United States Holocaust Memorial Museum, and the Holocaust Memorial Center Zekelman Family Campus.

Each of their stories is unique and as Alford (2015) argues, based on viewing 250 hours of interviews at the Fortunoff Video Archives for Holocaust Testimony at Yale, Survivors' stories

> ...are for the most part remarkably narratively com-
> petent – the stories are told with a beginning, middle
> and end, the narrators moving back and forth in time
> and space between here and now and there and then.
> Their affect is appropriate. In this respect the sur-
> vivors do not seem deeply traumatized.... Yet this
> narrative competence ... their ability to put words to
> the most terrible and traumatic experiences, did not

31

relieve them of their trauma. Instead, it seemed to
enable them to live alongside their trauma…. They
live a double existence ... where Holocaust memories
and normal memories are assigned to two, sometimes
hostile territories. (Alford, 2015, p. 267)

For others, artistic expression helps them achieve a sense of coherence and facilitates their healing and transformation and, as their art is experienced, it may contribute to collective healing (Corley, 2010). Others may help themselves through altruistic or contributory helping of others (Midlarsky & Kahana, 2007). Renewed religiousness and return to traditional rituals in aging Survivors may have an integrative function, in nostalgically attempting to recreate order, structure, and continuity with the pre-Holocaust past. Building monuments also serves the reestablishment of a sense of continuity for the Survivors and for the world. In addition to commemoration, it also serves the significant function of documentation – an extension of bearing witness and of leaving a legacy so that the victims, the Survivors, and the Holocaust will not be forgotten (Danieli, 1994). Through these private and public actions, they are able to release their traumatic memories and make them more available for conscious working through either on their own, with their family and friends, or with professional counseling and support to help them find a very personal meaning with their Holocaust trauma and transform a personal tragedy into a triumph.

Trauma and Its Effects on the Second and Third Generations
The consequences of traumatic events are not limited to the Adult and Child Survivors immediately exposed to the event. They often affect significant others in their environment such as family, friends, and caregivers, especially the "Second Generation" (2G) or the Offspring of Holocaust Survivors (OHS), and the "Third Generation" (3G) or Grandchildren of Holocaust Survivors (GHS), who may suffer

emotional disturbances, nightmares, anxiety, fear, and anger because of the experiences of their parents or grandparents. However, not only the trauma but also the survival and hope can be transmitted (Meyers, 2012). Survivors can communicate and model astounding strength, courage, and resilience for their children and grandchildren (Richman, 2012).

How is Trauma Transmitted?

While there is ongoing debate on whether trauma transmits through genetics, neurology, or interpersonal relations between parent and child, common knowledge dictates that children and grandchildren's worldviews are deeply affected by familial tragedies (Sapiro, 2012). Specific manifestations of trauma transmission can be explained as being determined by any or all of a complex of multiple related factors: *psychodynamic* – focus on unconscious and direct effects of parents on their children; *sociocultural* – emphasis on conscious and direct effects of parents on their children; *family system* – impact of family environment on the unconscious and conscious transmission of parental traumatization; and *biological* – health of the mother at the time of the birth, as well as genetic and/or biochemical predisposition to illness; or by an ecological combination of these (Kellermann, 2009).

Epigeneticists, who study how experience modifies expressions of phenotypes and gene expressions without changing the DNA sequence itself, explain how parental or familial trauma can change and alter the genetic landscape for generations to come. Such biological variations stemming from stress exposure in parents via changes to gametes and the gestational uterine environment or via early postnatal care has been referred to as "intergenerational transmission" (Bowers & Yehuda, 2016). The etiology of this transmission continues to be investigated, within the constraints related to the study of human subjects (Bowers & Yehuda, 2016; Yehuda & Lehrner, 2018).

Neuroscientists demonstrate how the brain can be rewired and neural connections changed after traumatic experiences to react to the world differently, thus influencing parental behavior, which in turn affects their child's personality development and attachment styles (Sapiro, 2012).

Attachment theorists suggest that parental anxiety affects the delicate bond of attachment between parents and their children, possibly leaving the children vulnerable and insecure. Alford explains that, "Children want and need to experience their parents' trauma.... To be excluded from their parents' subjectivity is as damaging as being overwhelmed by unintegrated parental experience" (Alford, 2015, p. 261).

The impact of the family environment cannot be overstated. As discovered by Yael Danieli, a clinical psychologist, victimologist, traumatologist, and the Director of the Group Project for Holocaust Survivors and their Children in New York, Holocaust parents to varying degrees transmitted to their children a sense of the conditions under which they had survived the war. In trying to cope, Survivors created families that tended to exhibit at least four differing post-war adaptational styles: (1) the *victim* families, characterized by pervasive depression, worry, mistrust, and fear of the outside world and by symbiotic clinging within the family; (2) *fighter* families, whose home atmosphere is permeated by an intense drive to build and achieve and is filled with compulsive activity; (3) *numb* families, characterized by pervasive silence and depletion of all emotions; and (4) families of *"those who made it,"* motivated by a wartime fantasy to "make it big" if they were liberated in order to defeat the Nazis (Danieli, 1981; Danieli, 1988, as described in Danieli, 2009). A follow-up study found that what mattered was the offspring-reported intensities of their mother's and father's victims' styles and suggested that survivors' and offspring's suffering might be reduced through efforts to recapture meaning, purpose, identity, connectedness of past, present, and future, and attachments to community and place (Danieli, Norris, & Engdahl,

2016).

Based on twenty years of intense qualitative research with Survivors and family members, the Transcending Trauma Project (TTP) found that the differences among families and how they nurture and socialize children in the formative years helps to explain variations in later adult coping and adaptation (Hollander-Goldfein et al., 2012). Hollander-Goldfein et al. (2012) described four categories of families: positive, negative, mixed, and mediated: 1) The parents who were able to protect and support their children's needs first and focus less on their own needs could provide the nurture and responsiveness that the children needed to develop in healthy ways while acknowledging their parents' difficulties and challenges; 2) On the other hand, Survivor families with predominantly negative relationships tended to display emotional difficulties in the second generation; 3) Families with mixed patterns resulted in a complex interplay of positive qualities and emotional difficulties for the children; and lastly, 4) The TTP found that the existence of even one healthier parent who succeeded in mitigating the negative impact of the emotionally distressed parent on the children could provide the children with the psychological tools to feel good about themselves, to engage in healthy adult relationships, to successfully nurture their children, and to succeed in life.

Whether hereditary or environmentally inflicted, the offspring of Holocaust Survivors, by the very fact that they have vicariously experienced so much tragedy, may also have been provided with some adaptive coping capability and with survival skills. They seem to struggle with stress and resilience at the same time and will have periods when one or the other is more dominant (Kellermann, 2009). Dr. Gita Arian Baack, born in a Displaced Persons camp to Holocaust Survivors, calls this secondary form of trauma "inherited trauma" and defines "inheritors" as the generations of people who, consciously or unconsciously, have thoughts and feelings about devastating events that happened when they were very young or before they were born, or that may even go back to earlier generations (Baack, 2017, p. 3). Her work with inheritors from families who lived through war, slavery, displacement, and many other kinds of family and community trauma also demonstrates that "if you have inherited trauma, you have also inherited the resilience to thrive, function successfully and make a difference on improving the human condition" (Baack, 2017, p. 6).

Israeli author Nava Semel comes from a "silent family" and calls those who have the traumatic event registered in their consciousness without actually having experienced it themselves "remembearers" "for they must bear the burden of memory" and the chain of remembe[a] rers who pass on the torch from hand to hand as in an Olympic relay race "memory carriers" (Semel, 2013). She believes in the power of the arts to fight against forgetfulness and denial. "Art can pass on the emotional memory to those who follow us. A story, a poem, a movie, a play, painting, music and dance are the best carriers of a memory that goes beyond the facts and events themselves. Art encapsulates the fate of one individual and can resurrect his story at the unparalleled time in human history" (Semel, 2013, pp. 90-91).

The son of Holocaust survivors, Lev Raphael is a pioneer in writing fiction about America's Second Generation. In his memoir "My Germany," he writes: "The camps and killing squads not only murdered dozens of my parents' relatives but also poisoned their memories. Poisoned mine. Talking about their lost parents, cousins, aunts, and uncles was so painful for my own parents that I have no family tree to climb in middle age, no names and professions and cities to study and explore." Yet, his mother told him "she never blamed all Germans, and that younger Germans surely had nothing to do with events before their birth" and when he finally went to Germany, it was not "to forgive anyone, but to explore what has always been taboo and terrifying to me. To face my demons" (Raphael, 2009, pp. 4-6).

Secondary and Tertiary Traumatization in the Research Literature

While the attitudes, behavior, and pathologies of the Survivors affect the worldview of their children and grandchildren, reviews of the research literature on children of Holocaust Survivors showed no evidence for the influence of the Survivor parents' traumatic Holocaust experiences on their children. Secondary traumatization emerged only in studies on clinical participants who were stressed by other psychological or physical adversities unrelated to the Holocaust (Kellermann, 2001; van IJzendoorn, Bakermans-Kranenburg, & Sagi-Schwartz, 2003). However, "even if not fully aware of it, they may have inherited an *existential angst* from the Holocaust in which the themes of death and survival are always present" (Kellermann, 2009, p. 99). Protective factors in the children or in their environment may have lessened the impact of their parents' trauma. But under conditions of extreme stress, latent vulnerability to maladaptive and prolonged posttraumatic responses may come to the surface (van IJzendoorn et al., 2003).

As an example, following the 1973 Yom Kippur War, Second Generation veterans with no psychopathology prior to the war reported less posttraumatic growth than veterans who were not Second Generation (Dekel, Mandl, & Solomon, 2013). This suggests that transgenerational transmission of trauma may limit offspring's positive adaptation following trauma.

An interesting and significant difference in the strength of Jewish identity that parents were able to pass down to their children was found between Second Generation children born to "older Survivors" who grew to adulthood during the 1960s and the children of Child Survivors who came of age during the 1980s, when even the nature of society was vastly different. Older Second Generation members were born to parents "with significant amounts of prewar Jewish learning from years of study and home life. Their powerful memories of tradition and family could be resuscitated in post war life and passed onto family."

37

But those who are Child Survivors "had fewer years in which to establish the necessary building blocks to a fully Jewish existence and had virtually no prewar life or early Jewish experiences in conscious awareness" (Krell, 2013, p.2). Indeed, many did not even know they were Jewish and had to struggle to forge that identity.

In studies involving the Third Generation, there also was no evidence of tertiary traumatization (Sagi-Schwartz, van IJzendoorn, & Bakermans-Kranenburg, 2008). Protective factors included that the traumatic experiences of the Survivors were not inflicted by their own parents or other attachment figures, that secure attachment relationships had been established before the war between Survivors and their own parents or other attachment figures, that Holocaust Survivors were not genetically biased to develop intense posttraumatic stress reactions, and that social support was available to cope with the trauma afterwards (Sagi-Schwartz et al., 2008).

In another study of intergenerational transmission of trauma among the Second and Third Generations, Giladi and Bell (2013) suggest a mixture of resilience and vulnerability factors, with greater differentiation of self and better family communication associated with lower levels of secondary traumatic stress. Palgi, Shrira, and Ben-Ezra (2015) also found that family involvement serves as an important mechanism of the intergenerational transmission of Holocaust trauma to Offspring of Holocaust Survivors and Grandchildren of Holocaust Survivors and that it was associated with a higher level of preoccupation with Holocaust contents.

Moreover, the provocative idea that trauma might skip a generation has not been supported (Sagi-Schwartz et al., 2008). This may be due to the fact that the second generation "grew up at a time when Holocaust Survivors were shunned in society, [while] grandchildren of survivors grew up at a time in society when Holocaust Survivors had regained their sense of dignity . . . a transformation from shame to pride" (Eva Fogelman, as cited in Nathan-Kazis, 2012). In addition, the special communication between the grandchildren and grandparents has helped to transform their most traumatic events into something to be proud of (Kellermann, 2009), and "how to be in the world" (Hollander-Goldfein et. al., 2012, p. 223).

In their recent study of Grandchildren of Holocaust Survivors in Australia (2018), Cohn and Morrison found that the lived experiences of the Third Generation are heavily influenced by their active connection with the Holocaust. These individuals have sought knowledge and understanding of their grandparents' experiences by avenues additional to grandparent narratives, therefore overcoming the 'conspiracy of silence' evident in their parents' often more passive Holocaust exposure. Furthermore, the participants' accounts suggest that their families' Holocaust histories provide them with an ethical framework in relation to the contemporary suffering of other groups and to value social justice.

Lessons Learned

I also suffered the loss of many family members who remained in Vilna, Lithuania, during the Holocaust. The few who survived inspired me to study the human impact of traumatic events, such as the Holocaust and other genocides, terrorism (Konvisser, 2006, 2013, 2014, 2016a), combat (Konvisser, 2016b), and wrongful conviction (Konvisser, 2012, 2015, 2017, forthcoming), which can be described as a struggle – and often a battle – with highly challenging life circumstances and how we must move forward from and learn to live beyond the trauma.

My passion is to give voice to these trauma survivors by listening to and documenting their "stories" – their oral histories or testimonies – as a gift to them and their families and as a way of remembering and learning from their experiences. While death and distress are all too present in these stories, they also emphasize that hope and meaning can be found after struggling with and surviving any life crisis. While they do not forget their traumatic experiences, many survivors are able to integrate and own the painful emotions of their situation, make them part of their story, and live with them in a productive way. Like trees that bend or change shape to accommodate the wind, they are able to recover or even reconfigure their lives and have learned how to *live next to* and *move forward* with their feelings of grief, pain, and helplessness.

My mother's cousin, Izaak Wirszup, lived through the Vilna Ghetto and the concentration camps and came out believing that he was spared in order to make a difference. Out of his struggle came a Survivor's love of life and a legacy. Izaak expressed it this way:

> When you alone remain alive, you have to justify
> yourself. We have seen firsthand the desecration of
> life. We have witnessed the organized annihilation
> of millions of innocent wonderful human beings. We
> have seen giants collapse – morally and physically –
> within days, when subjected to inhuman onditions.
> But we have also encountered people who would
> make any sacrifice; heroes whose like we had seen
> before only in the scriptures. We have seen how Ho-
> locaust Survivors and their descendants can transform
> the most fragile souls into individuals stronger than
> steel (Harms, 1996, p. 37).

As described in this chapter, there exist an almost infinite number of identifiable forces and factors that interact with each other in an almost infinite number of ways to shape or determine the long-term effect on any particular individual of the Holocaust and similar atrocities wherein the threat to physical survival or well-being is prominent – victims of genocides, hatred, torture, or other oppressions. While each experience is unique, by bringing forth and understanding some of the common qualities and sources of strength that help people cope with the tragedy and uncertainty and survive the long-term impacts of extreme prolonged trauma, we provide valuable insights and evidence for the traumatized individuals themselves; for their families, friends, and communities supporting their recovery; for clinicians and counselors developing treatment modalities; and for policy-makers and advocates of social justice providing interventions that could not only mitigate the negative effects of these horrific traumatic events, but also help foster more positive, long-term adaptations for the Survivors (see also Hollander-Goldfein et al., 2012).

And, as so eloquently expressed by Elie Wiesel, Holocaust survivor, Nobel Poet Laureate, and Founding Chairman of the United States Holocaust Memorial Museum at the dedication ceremonies of the U.S. Holocaust Memorial Museum: "For the dead and the living, we must bear witness. For not only are we responsible for the memories of the dead, we are also responsible for what we are doing with those memories" (Wiesel, April 22, 1993).

References

Alford, C. F. (2015). Subjectivity and the intergenerational transmission of historical trauma: Holocaust survivors and their children. *Subjectivity, 8*, 261–282. doi:10.1057/sub.2015.10

American Psychological Association (2010). *The road to resilience.* Washington, DC: American Psychological Association. Retrieved from http://www.apa.org/helpcenter/road-resilience.aspx

Amir, M., & Lev-Wiesel, R. (2001). Secondary traumatic stress, psychological distress, sharing of traumatic reminiscences and marital quality among spouses of Holocaust child survivors. *Journal of Marital and Family Therapy, 27,* 297-108.

Armour, M. (2010) Meaning making in survivorship: Application to Holocaust survivors. *Journal of Human Behavior in the Social Environment, 20*(4), 440-468. doi:10.1080/10911350903274997

Baack, G. A. (2017). *The Inheritors: Moving forward from generational trauma.* Berkeley, CA: She Writes Press.

Barak, Y. (2013). Aging of child Holocaust survivors. *Kavod 3*. Retrieved September 25, 2018 from the World Wide Web: http://kavod.claimscon.org/2013/02/aging-child-survivors/

Barel, E., van IJzendoorn, M. H., Sagi-Schwartz, A., & Bakermans-Kranenburg, M. J. (2010). Surviving the Holocaust: A meta-analysis of the long-term sequelae of a genocide. *Psychological Bulletin, 136*:5, 677-698.

Bar-On, D., Eland, J., Kleber, R.J., Krell, R., Moore, Y., Sagi, A., Soriano, E., Suedfeld, P., van-der-Velden, P.G., & van IJzendoorn, M. H. (1998). Multigenerational perspective on coping with the Holocaust experience: An attachment perspective for understanding the development sequel of trauma across generations. *International Journal of Behavioral Development, 22,* 315-338.

Berger, A. L. & Berger, N. (2001). *Second generation voices: Reflections by children of Holocaust survivors & perpetrators.* Syracuse, NY: Syracuse University Press.

Bowers, M. E. & Yehuda, R. (2016). Intergenerational transmission of stress in humans. *Neuropsychopharmacology Reviews, 41,* 232–244. doi:10.1038/npp.2015.247

Butler, L. D., Morland, L. A., & Leskin, G. A. (2006). Psychological resilience in the face of terrorism. In B. Bongar, L. Beutler, P. G. Zimbardo, L. M. Brown & J. N. Breckenridge (Eds.), *Psychology of terrorism* (pp. 400-417). New York, NY: Oxford University Press.

Calhoun, L. G., & Tedeschi, R. G. (2006). *Handbook of posttraumatic growth: Research and practice.* Mahwah, NJ: Lawrence Erlbaum.

Carver, C. S. (1998). Resilience and thriving: Issues, models, and linkages. *Journal of Social Issues, 54*(2), 245-266.

Clementi, F. K. (2013). *Holocaust mothers & daughters: Family, histo-*

ry and trauma. Lebanon, NH: Brandeis University Press.

Cohen, M., Brom, D., & Dasberg, H. (2001). Child survivors of the Holocaust: symptoms and coping after fifty years. *The Israel Journal of Psychiatry and Related Sciences, 38*(1), 3-12.

Cohn, I. G. & Morrison, N. M. V. (2018). Echoes of transgenerational trauma in the lived experiences of Jewish Australian grandchildren of Holocaust survivors. *Australian Journal of Psychology, 70*, 199–207. doi: 10.1111/ajpy.12194

Corley, C. (2010). Creative expression and resilience among Holocaust survivors. *Journal of Human Behavior in the Social Environment, 20*, 542-552.

Danieli, Y. (1981). On the achievement of integration in aging survivors of the Nazi Holocaust. *Journal of Geriatric Psychiatry, 14*(2), 191-210.

Danieli, Y. (1985). The treatment and prevention of long-term effects and intergenerational transmission of victimization: a lesson from Holocaust survivors and their children. In C. R. Figley (Ed.), *Trauma and its wake* (pp. 295-313). New York, NY: Brunner/Mazel.

Danieli, Y. (1988). On not confronting the Holocaust: Psychological reactions to victim/survivors and their children. In *Remembering for the future, Theme 2: The impact of the Holocaust on the contemporary world* (pp. 1257-1271). Oxford: Pergamon Press.

Danieli, Y. (1994). As survivors age: Part 1. *National Center for PTSD Clinical Quarterly, 4*(1), 1-7.

Danieli, Y. (2009, Winter). Conspiracy of silence: A conversation with Dr. Yael Danieli. *Reform Judaism Magazine*, 51-53.

Danieli, Y., Norris, F. H., & Engdahl, B. (2016, January 14). Multigenerational legacies of trauma: Modeling the what and how of transmission. *American Journal of Orthopsychiatry*. Advance online publication. http://dx.doi.org/10.1037/ort0000145

David, P. (2011). *Aging Holocaust survivors: An evolution of under-standing*. Kavod – Honoring Aging Survivors. Retrieved October 11, 2012, 2012, from the World Wide Web: http://kavod.claimscon.org/2010/09/aging-holocaust-survivors-an-evolution-of-understanding/

David, P. & Pelly, S. (Eds.) (2003). *Caring for aging Holocaust survivors: A practice manual*. Toronto: Baycrest Centre for Geriatric Care.

Dekel, S., Mandl, C., & Solomon, Z. (2013). Is the Holocaust implicated in posttraumatic growth in second-generation Holocaust survivors? A prospective study. *Journal of Traumatic Stress, 26*(4), 530-533.

Epstein, H. (1979). *Children of the Holocaust: Conversations with sons and daughters of survivors*. New York: NY: Penguin Books.

Feldman, M., Taieb, O., & Moro, M. R. (2010). Jewish children hidden in France between 1940 and 1944. *American Journal of Orthopsychiatry, 80*(4), 547-556.

Frank, A. (February 23, 1944). *The diary of a young girl*. Retrieved October 14, 2018 from the World Wide Web: https://books.google.com/books?id=Q85EDwAAQBAJ&lpg=PT132&dq=diary%20of%20a%20young%20girl%20chestnut%20tree%2C%20on%20whose%20branches%20little%20raindrops%20shine%2C%20appear%20like%20silver.&pg=PT132#v=onepage&q=diary%20of%20a%20young%20girl%20chestnut%20tree,%20on%20whose%20branches%20little%20raindrops%20shine,%20appear%20like%20silver.&f=false

Frankl, V. E. (2006). *Man's search for meaning* (I. Lasch, Trans.). Boston, MA: Beacon Press.

Fridman, A., Bakermans-Kranenburg, M. J., Sagi-Schwartz, A., & van IJzendoorn, M. H. (2011). Coping in old age with extreme childhood trauma: Aging Holocaust survivors and their offspring facing new challenges. *Aging & Mental Health, 15*:2, 232-242.

Garwood, A. (1996). The Holocaust and the power of powerlessness: Survivor guilt, an unhealed wound. *British Journal of Psychotherapy, 13*:2, 243-258.

Giladi, L. & Bell, T. S. (2013). Protective Factors for Intergenerational Transmission of Trauma Among Second and Third Generation Holocaust Survivors. *Psychological Trauma: Theory, Research, Practice, and Policy, 5*(4), 384–391.

Greene, R. R. (2002). Holocaust Survivors, *Journal of Gerontological Social Work, 37*(1), 3-18.

Greene, R. R. (Ed.) (2010). *Studies of the Holocaust: Lessons in Survivorship.* New York, NY: Routledge.

Greene, R. R. & Graham, S. A. (2009). Role of resilience among Nazi Holocaust survivors: A strength-based paradigm for understanding survivorship. *Family & Community Health, 32*(1), S75-S82. doi: 10.1097/01.FCH.0000342842.51348.83

Harms, W. (Oct-Dec 1996). The Wirszup Factor. *University of Chicago Magazine,* 34-37.

Helmreich, W. B. (1992). *Against all odds: Holocaust survivors and the successful lives they made in America.* New York, NY: Simon & Schuster.

Herman, J. L. (1997). *Trauma and recovery: The aftermath of violence from domestic abuse to political terror* (Rev. ed.). New York, NY: BasicBooks.

Hollander-Goldfein, B., Isserman, N., & Goldenberg, J. (2012). *Transcending trauma: Survival, resilience, and clinical implications in survivor families.* New York, NY: Routledge.

Isserman, Nancy & Hollander-Goldfein, Bea & Nechama Horwitz, S. (2016). Challenges for aging Holocaust survivors and their children: The impact of early trauma on aging. *Journal of Religion, Spirituality & Aging,* 1-25. doi:10.1080/15528030.201

6.1193094.

Janoff-Bulman, R. (1992). *Shattered assumptions: towards a new psychology of trauma.* New York, NY: Free Press.

Joseph, S., & Dr. Linley, P. A. (2008). *Trauma, recovery, and growth: positive psychological perspectives on posttraumatic stress.* Hoboken, NJ: John Wiley.

Kahana, E., & Kahana, B. (2001). *Meeting challenges of aging among elderly survivors of the Nazi Holocaust.* Paper presented at the 35th World Congress of the International Institute of Sociology, Krakow, Poland.

Kahana, B., Harel, Z., & Kahana, E. (2010). *Holocaust survivors and immigrants: Late life adaptations.* New York, NY: Springer.

Kellermann, N. P. F. (2001). Psychopathology in children of Holocaust survivors: A review of the research literature. *Israel Journal of Psychiatry and Related Sciences, 38*(1), 36-46.

Kellermann, N. P. F. (2009). *Holocaust trauma: Psychological effects and treatment.* New York, NY: Bloomington.

Konvisser, Z. L. (2006). *Finding meaning and growth in the aftermath of suffering: Israeli civilian survivors of suicide bombings and other attacks.* (Doctoral dissertation). Retrieved from https://fgul.idm.oclc.org/docview/304914620?accountid=10868

Konvisser, Z. D. (2012). Psychological consequences of wrongful conviction in women and the possibility of positive change. *DePaul University College of Law, Center for Public Interest Law's Journal for Social Justice, 5*(2) 221-94.

Konvisser, Z. D. (2013). Themes of resilience and growth in survivors of politically motivated violence. *Traumatology, XX*(X), 1-11.

Konvisser, Z. D. (2014). *Living beyond terrorism: Israeli stories of hope and healing.* Jerusalem: Gefen.

Konvisser, Z. D. (2015). "What happened to me can happen to anybody" – Women exonerees speak out. *Texas A&M Law Re-*

view, *3*, 303-366.

Konvisser, Z. D. (2016a). *From terror to meaning and healing – A Franklian view. The International Forum for Logotherapy, 39*, *22-27*.

Konvisser, Z. D. (2016b). Healing returning veterans: The role of storytelling and community, *Veteran and Family Reintegration: Identity, Healing, and Reconciliation* (Fielding Monograph Series, Volume 8).

Konvisser, Z. D. (2017). Exoneree engagement in policy reform work: An exploratory study of the Innocence Movement policy reform process. *Journal of Contemporary Criminal Justice, 33*(1), 43-60. doi: 10.1177/1043986216673010

Konvisser, Z. D. (forthcoming). Transforming the trauma of wrongful conviction: Women exonerees in the Innocence Movement. In Coping with liminality through communitas: Experiences of collective transformation in the midst of discomforting transitions, *Journal of Transformative Education*.

Krell, R. (1995). Children who survived the Holocaust: Reflections of a child survivor/psychiatrist. *Echoes of the Holocaust*.

Krell, R. (2012). *Thirty years of friendship, healing & education – Our legacy.* Paper presented at the World Federation of Jewish Child Survivors of the Holocaust and Descendants, Cleveland, Ohio.

Krell, R. (Spring, 2013). 30 years of friendship, healing & education – Our legacy. *Mishpocha!*, p. 2. Newsletter of the World Federation of Jewish Child Survivors of the Holocaust and Descendants.

Lepore, S. J., & Revenson, T. A. (2006). *Resilience and posttraumatic growth: Recovery, resistance, and reconfiguration.* In L. G. Calhoun & R. G. Tedeschi, pp. 24-30.

Lessing, F. (February 28, 2013). Personal communication.

Lev-Wiesel, R. & Amir, M. (2003). Posttraumatic growth among Holocaust child survivors. *Journal of Loss and Trauma, 8*(4), 229-237.

Meyers, M. B. (2012). Trauma, therapy, and witnessing. In N. R. Goodman & M. B. Meyers (Eds.), *The power of witnessing: Reflections, reverberations, and traces of the Holocaust,* (pp. 289-303). New York, NY: Taylor & Francis.

Midlarsky, E., & Kahana, E. (2007). Altruism, well-being, and mental health in late life. In S. G. Post (Ed.), *Altruism and health: Perspectives from empirical research,* (pp. 56-69). New York, NY: Oxford University Press.

Nathan-Kazis, J. (September 7, 2012). Can Holocaust trauma pass to third generation? *Forward, 116,* 1.

Palgi, Y., Shrira, A., & Ben-Ezra, M. (2015). Family involvement and Holocaust salience among offspring and grandchildren of Holocaust survivors, *Journal of Intergenerational Relationships, 13*(1), 6-21. doi: 10.1080/15350770.2015.992902

Quarantelli, E.L. (1985). An assessment of conflicting views on mental health: the consequences of traumatic events. In Figley, C.R. (ed.) *Trauma and its wake: The study and treatment of posttraumatic stress disorder* (Vol. 1b, pp. 173-218). New York, NY: Brunner/Mazel.

Raphael, L. (2009). *My Germany: A Jewish writer returns to the world his parents escaped.* Madison, WI: Terrace Books.

Richman, S. (2012). "Too young to remember": Recovering and integrating the unacknowledged known. In N. R. Goodman & M. B. Meyers (Eds.), *The power of witnessing: Reflections, reverberations, and traces of the Holocaust,* (pp. 105-18). New York, NY: Taylor & Francis.

Rosensaft, M. Z. (Ed.) (2015). *God, faith & identity from the ashes: Reflections of children and grandchildren of Holocaust survivors.* Woodstock, VT: Jewish Lights Publishing.

Sagi-Schwartz, A., van IJzendoorn, M. H., & Bakermans-Kranenburg, M. (2008). Does intergenerational transmission of trauma skip a generation? No meta-analytic evidence for tertiary traumatization with third generation of Holocaust survivors. *Attachment & Human Development, 10*(2), 105-121.

Sagi-Schwartz, A., Bakermans-Kranenburg, M. J., Linn, S., & van IJzendoorn, M. H. (2013). *Against all odds: Genocidal trauma is associated with longer life-expectancy of the survivors.* PLoS ONE *8*(7): e69179. doi:10.1371/journal.pone.0069179

Sapiro, M. (2012). Intergenerational transmission of trauma: How the Holocaust transmits and affects child development. *Hadassah-Brandeis Institute Project on Families, Children and the Holocaust Working Papers Series.* Waltham, MA: Brandeis University. http://www.brandeis.edu/hbi/childrenholocaust/workingpapers/index.html

Semel, N. (2013). Memory's children. *Trauma and Memory 1*:2, 88-91. doi: 10.12869/TM2013-2-04

Southwick, S. M., Vythilingam, M., & Charney, D. S. (2005). The psychobiology of depression and resilience to stress: Implications for prevention and treatment. *Annual Review of Clinical Psychology, 1*, 255-291.

Southwick, S. M., & Charney, D. S. (2012). *Resilience: The science of mastering life's greatest challenges.* New York, NY: Cambridge University Press.

Tedeschi, R. G., & Calhoun, L. G. (1995). *Trauma & transformation: Growing in the aftermath of suffering.* Thousand Oaks, CA: SAGE.

Tedeschi, R. G., & Calhoun, L. G. (2004a). Posttraumatic growth: A new perspective on psychotraumatology. *Psychiatric Times, XXI*(4), 58.

Tedeschi, R. G., & Calhoun, L. G. (2004b). Posttraumatic growth: Conceptual foundations and empirical evidence. *Psychologi-*

cal Inquiry, 15(1), 1-18.

van IJzendoorn, M. H., Bakermans-Kranenburg, M. J., & Sagi-Schwartz, A. (2003). Are children of Holocaust survivors
less well-adapted? A meta-analytic investigation of secondary
traumatization. *Journal of Traumatic Stress, 16*(5), 459-469.

Vaillant, G. E. (2002). *Aging well.* New York, NY: Little, Brown and
Company.

Wiesel, E. (April 22, 1993). *Remarks at the dedication ceremonies for
the United States Holocaust Memorial Museum.* Retrieved
from the World Wide Web: https://www.ushmm.org/informa-
tion/about-the-museum/mission-and-history/wiesel

Wohlleben, P. (2016). *The hidden life of trees: What they feel, how they
communicate – Discoveries from a secret world.* Vancouver,
BC: Greystone Books.

Yehuda, R. & Lehrner, A. (2018). Intergenerational transmission of
trauma effects: putative role of epigenetic mechanisms. *World
Psychiatry. 17*(3), 243-257. doi: 10.1002/wps.20568

About the Author

Zieva Dauber Konvisser, PhD is a Fellow of the Institute for Social
Innovation at Fielding Graduate University and an Adjunct Assistant
Professor of Criminal Justice at Wayne State University. Her research
and writing focus on the human impact of traumatic events, including
terrorism, genocide, combat, and wrongful conviction. Her passion
is to collect and share the oral histories or testimonies of survivors
of traumas to make known the human "stories" behind the headlines.
She volunteers as the Oral Historian at the Holocaust Memorial Center
Zekelman Family Campus, served on the National Commission on
American Jewish Women, and serves on the boards of METIV: The
Israel Psychotrauma Center of Herzog Hospital, Strength to Strength,

and Proving Innocence. Her publications include: *Themes of Resilience and Growth in Survivors of Politically Motivated Violence* (2013*)*; *Psychological Consequences of Wrongful Conviction in Women and the Possibility of Positive Change* (2012); *"What Happened to Me Can Happen to Anybody"* – *Women Exonerees Speak Out* (2015); *From Terror to Meaning and Healing – A Franklian View (2016); Healing Returning Veterans: The Role of Storytelling and Community* (2016); *Exoneree Engagement in Policy Reform Work: An Exploratory Study of the Innocence Movement Policy Reform Process* (2017); and *Living Beyond Terrorism: Israeli Stories of Hope and Healing* (2014). Dr. Konvisser may be contacted at zkonvisser@comcast.net or by visiting her website at www.zievakonvisser.com.

CHAPTER 2

TRAJECTORIES OF RESILIENCE FOR WHISTLEBLOWER PSYCHOLOGICAL TRAUMA

Rebecca Stafford
Fellow, Institute for Social Innovation, Fielding Graduate University
Andrea Meier
Flourish! Personal Coaching

Abstract

Trauma refers to the experiences that cause intense physical and psychological stress reactions which have lasting adverse effects on the individual's physical, social, emotional, and spiritual well-being (Janoff-Bulman, 2002). That said, many trauma survivors do demonstrate emotional resilience. They possess the capacity to go on with life after experiencing hardship and adversity. They seek ways to recover their levels of pretrauma adaptation (Tedeschi & Calhoun, 2004) and to regain and maintain relatively stable levels of psychological and physical functioning (Bonanno, 2004). This chapter reviews the characteristics of whistleblowers, the act of whistleblowing, and the traumas caused by employer retaliation. It situates whistleblowing within the larger context of psychological traumatization and examines the impacts of such traumatization on memory and behavior. To illustrate whistleblower resilience, it draws on Stafford's (2017) mixed-method study of whistleblowers who were targets of employer retaliation, and who experienced psychological traumatization. Stafford found all that all her participants demonstrated resilience, but that their resilience strategies involved a variety of types of coping behaviors and therapeutic supports to enable them to survive in their toxic workplaces. In the final section, we review promising trauma-informed psychotherapies that can reduce the length of time to recovery and the achievement of wellbeing.

Keywords: psychological trauma, whistleblowers, resilience, posttraumatic growth, coping behavior, treatments for psychological trauma

Introduction

Resilience constitutes the human drive to go on with life after experiencing hardship and adversity. After devastating events, it involves the thoughts, feelings, and behaviors that motivate effort to return to pre-trauma levels of adaptation (Tedeschi & Calhoun, 2004) and to regain and maintain relatively stable levels of psychological and physical functioning (Bonanno, 2004). Evidence of posttrauma resilience crosses multiple life domains (Kira, Ashby, Omidy, & Lewandowski, 2015). These include: (1) restoration of pretrauma levels of health and adoption of wellbeing promoting behaviors, (2) forward seeking motivation to reengage with life, (3) reclaiming positive identity that includes positive self-concept, self-esteem, and self-efficacy, (4) engaging in self-reflection that promotes self-awareness and a coherent trauma narrative; (5) cognitive meta-processing of events to support emotional regulation and effective coping; and (6) increased stress tolerance coupled with an understanding about how stressors in different parts of life can feed back on each other. Most trauma-informed therapies address the individual and interpersonal levels of resolution of trauma experiences. As healing at that level progresses, trauma survivors may choose to become advocates, working with groups and institution, to seek justice for other victims and change the conditions that allowed the traumas to happen in the first place.

Whistleblowers and Whistleblowing

This chapter examines the efforts of public leader whistleblowers, who were targets of traumatizing employer retaliation, to recover their lives. Whistleblowers are employees within organizations who have witnessed corruption in the form of unethical, immoral, and/or illegal workplace infractions and who have attempted to put an end to such activities by reporting them to the authorities. Because whistleblowing threatens established corrupt power structures within organizations, whistleblowers are often targets for retaliation by their superiors or others whose power and status are threatened. Employer retaliation after a whistleblower has publicly exposed illegitimate organizational activities has legal standing and justifies criminal prosecution (Hamid & Othman, 2015; Sonnier & Lasser, 2013; U.S. Equal Employment Opportunity Commission, n.d.).

Whistleblowing is a personal response to institutional corruption. Corruption is defined as the abuse of entrusted power for private gain. Corruption can occur in corporate as well as government and community agencies. It can be classified as grand, petty, and political, depending on the amounts of money lost and the sector where it occurs (Transparency International, 2017). A 2017 Transparency International report conducted a telephone survey on perceptions of public corruption using a representative national sample of 1,007 U.S. residents (Transparency International, 2017). Researchers found that public perception is that corruption in public agencies is rampant. While 74 percent of survey respondents said that ordinary people can make a difference in fighting corruption, 55 percent listed fear of retaliation as the main reason for not whistleblowing. The frequency of this response was up from 31 percent in 2016.

Given the high risk for retaliation, what kinds of people are likely to become whistleblowers? In two large studies of Norwegian municipal employees (total N=2888), Bjørkelo and colleagues (Bjørkelo et al., 2010) investigated the relationship of personality traits to the likelihood of becoming a whistleblower. Across the two studies, nearly eight percent (n=294) of respondents had been whistleblowers once. Approximately an equal proportion had blown the whistle two or more times. Women were more likely than men to blow the whistle once. Men were more likely than women to blow the whistle more than once.

Whistleblowers tended to be more dominant and extroverted than non-whistleblowers. Extroverted individuals are likely to be verbal and sociable and prone to share their concerns about perceived wrongdoings. Dominant individuals tend to be more assertive than their peers and confident that their concerns will be heard. They may also be more staunch than other workers in resisting manipulation by management or other wrongdoers and more likely to persist in contesting issues of personal importance, continuing to report malfeasance over and over again if their reports are not heard or if they are retaliated against (Bjørkelo, Ryberg, & Einarsen, 2008; Stafford, 2017). Stafford's informants showed many of these same characteristics.

Characterizing Trauma

Trauma refers to experiences that cause intense physical and psychological stress reactions which have lasting adverse effects on the individual's physical, social, emotional, or spiritual well-being. Traumatic events are generally classified into three categories: (1) accidents, natural disasters, illness and injuries, (2) threats or harm to others, and (3) threats or harm to self. *Traumatization* may be experienced as one or many co-occurring emotional disorders that result from painful life altering events. These disorders include: (a) depressive disorders, (b) acute trauma-related stress disorders (TRSD), (c) anxiety, (d) generalized anxiety disorder, (e) panic disorders, (f) obsessive-compulsive disorders, and (g) posttraumatic stress disorder (PTSD).

PTSD is defined as the most extreme biopsychosocial manifestation of trauma impacts in individuals who are exposed to threatening life-altering events (Barsaglini, Sartori, Benetti, Pettersson-Yeo, & Mechelli, 2013). TRSD symptoms must persist for a minimum of one month to justify a diagnosis of PTSD. Either of these syndromes can result from brief, or enduring, or repeated traumatic experiences (Stein et al., 2014). However, the underlying neurobiology of traumatization in TRSD and PTSD differs in its expression, primarily in the duration, severity, and range of co-morbid symptoms, so we will refer to both as "traumatization" in the rest of this chapter.

Epidemiology of Trauma

Within the U.S. population as a whole, roughly 50 to 60 percent are exposed to some kind of significant, traumatizing stressor in their lifetimes (Ozer, Best, Lipsey, & Weiss, 2003). While TSRD is considered a less severe diagnosis than PTSD, studies of the clinical impacts of this disorder indicate that those diagnosed with it are three to five times more likely to see a physician, as well as six times more likely to be hospitalized for psychiatric disorders than those who are not afflicted with anxiety-related disorders (Bjørkelo, 2013, p. 281). PTSD affects approximately 7.7 million adults aged 18 and older (3.5 percent) in the U.S. (Anxiety and Depression Association of America, n.d.). It is a testimony to human resilience that only 5 to 10 percent of those people who have experienced some kind of traumatization have symptoms that persist long enough to be classified as PTSD (Ozer et al., 2003). Thus, despite such devastating experiences, a surprising proportion of trauma survivors demonstrate resilience and are able regain and maintain relatively stable levels of psychological and physical functioning (Bonanno, 2004; Galea, Nandi, & Vlahov, 2005).

Prevalence of whistleblower traumatizing events. While current statistics on retaliation are hard to find, a 2012 study by the Ethics Research Center found that 15 percent of whistleblowers reported that they were passed over for raises and promotions, and/or were relocated, reassigned, or demoted after they reported violations. Nearly a third of those who reported retaliation also experienced physical attacks or had their homes or cars damaged (Mont, 2012). Furthermore, however righteous the allegations, the lengthy, uncertain process of prosecuting such violations can be extremely costly in terms of health and wellbeing, personal relationships, job security and future prospects, personal and professional standing.

Psychological Traumatization. In this chapter, we will only address types of psychological traumatization in the context of whistleblowing. This aspect of traumatization occurs when an event or situation overwhelms the individual's ability to cope, leaving that person emotionally, cognitively, and physically devastated. The circumstances of such events often include abuse of power, betrayal of trust, entrapment, helplessness, pain, confusion, and loss. Even when there is no bodily injury, psychological trauma is often coupled with severe chronic stress resulting in physiological disruptions which further complicate recovery (Pearlman & Saakvitne, 1995).

Complex traumatization. Much trauma research has investigated the destructive effects of single event traumas. However, in life, traumas often occur as complex traumatic events and experiences become repetitive, prolonged, or cumulative over an extended period (Cortois & Ford, 2009). Most often these are interpersonal, involving direct harm, exploitation, or maltreatment. While they often occur at developmentally vulnerable times in the victim's life, especially in early childhood or adolescence, they can also occur later in life and in conditions of vulnerability associated with disability, disempowerment, dependency, age, or infirmity.

Whistleblower-specific traumas. For whistleblowers, the initial traumatizing event occurs when they first discover corruption.

Subsequent traumas may occur as they uncover its extent within the organization, the experiences of betrayals by coworkers to whom they confide the information, and the consequences that happen when they report it. Bjorkelo summarized four reasons for employer retaliatory acts: "Employers may be motivated by the organization's desire to (1) silence the whistleblower completely, (2) prevent a full public knowledge of the complaint, (3) discredit the whistleblower, and/ or (4) discourage other potential whistleblowers from taking action" (Bjørkelo, 2013, p 281).

Because they typically are confident, high performing, ethical professionals (Mesmer-Magnus & Viswesvaran, 2005), whistleblowers are blindsided by the small and large traumatizing events incurred by their employers' ongoing retaliation tactics. Therefore, for this population, we need to broaden the definition of complex traumatization. The informants in Stafford's study were targets of retaliation for years. As with other whistleblowers, they, too, were victims of personal attacks and many forms of disempowerment. However, their vulnerabilities were not due to the most common factors of age, disability, or dependency. Their vulnerabilities were, paradoxically, consequences of their strengths and their strong sense of ethics.

Trauma's Impacts on Memory and Behavior

Traumatic events cause disruptions in the brain's bio-chemical and electro-chemical processes which then cause changes in those brain structures that are the physiological basis of memory and learning. In order to understand how traumatization caused the biopsychosocial (BPS) impacts experienced by Stafford and her whistleblower participants, it is important to understand some basic neurobiology of memory and learning. This information is also important for understanding the various theoretical bases of the different trauma-focused therapies we describe in the final section.

Types of Memory

Memory is defined as all the ways that our experience of the world is encoded, stored, and later retrieved (Kandel & Schwartz, 1982). Learning results from the strengthening of existing encoded responses or the formation of new responses to existing stimuli that occurs because of practice or repetition (Mann, 2018). Within in this framework, traumatic events are powerful occasions for aversive learning. Resilience involves unlearning the BPS aspects of those traumatizing experiences. Memory, therefore, is not a "thing." It is a series of complex processes that progresses from instantaneous sensory impressions to long term memory storage (Atkinson & Shiffrin, 1968). There are two major types of memory: short- and long-term. Figure 1 diagrams the relationship and functions of each type and where they are stored in the brain.

Current research has identified the basic neural component of memory, engram cells, as enduring physical and/or chemical changes that are evoked by experience. These cells underlie the newly formed memory association. Memory recall is a function of reactivation of part of the original stimuli encoded during the original experience (Tonegawa, Liu, Ramirez, & Redondo, 2015). Engram cells for a given memory can be connected, directly or indirectly, to larger neuronal circuits. Memories are not stored in one place in the brain. They are stored in different locations depending on their sensory and emotional content. (See Figure 1.) Those brain areas interact with each other in complex ways to coordinate emotions, thoughts, and actions. Traumatic experiences cause dysregulation of these interactions thereby producing trauma symptoms

Short-Term Memory

Short-term memory (STM) storage begins as the mapping of encoded sensory perceptions in the brain's sensory cortex. Moments in time that interest us (i.e., activate the frontal lobes) or are emotionally arousing (i.e., stimulate cortisol production) are encoded and pass in less than a couple of seconds into the short-term memory circuits (van der Kolk, 1997). Only then are the actual sensations derived from the event processed. This process is called *synaptic consolidation.*

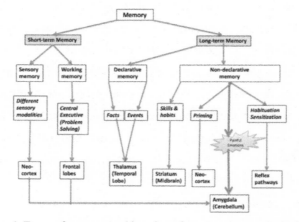

Figure 1. Types of memory and location of memory storage in the brain.

Under normal conditions, consolidation of "these sensory inputs are organized in a manner that enables an individual to establish a sense of where the body is in time and space, to feel safe in one's own body and to accurately perceive the body's relationship to the environment" (Kaiser, Gillette, & Spinazzola, 2010, p. 701). Trauma-related cortisol spiking can disrupt these synaptic consolidation processes. The emotional arousal caused by cortisol surges often evokes hyper-vigilance to potential threats. It can also prevent integration of sensory memories causing dissociation, the fragmentation of emotional, sensory, cognitive, and behavioral aspects of the traumatic memories stored at an unconscious level in the amygdala. Trauma survivors may experience this dissociation as depersonalization, derealization, altered time perception, and/or emotional numbing (Brewin, Gregory, Lipton, & Burgess, 2010).

Working Memory

Working memory is also part of the short-term memory system. Once sensory memories are encoded, they are sent on to different systems depending on the type of information being processed (Baddeley, 1986). For cognitive tasks and problem solving, signals are transmitted to the cerebral cortex. Emotions are regulated by another important midbrain area, the hippocampus, which also interacts with the frontal lobes, supporting--or interfering with—its executive control capacity. The emotional aspects of a traumatic event are processed via a strongly linked, unconscious pathway in the brain leading from the sensory cortex to the amygdala, causing amygdala hyper-activation and hippocampus hypo-activation. Chronic stress weakens connectivity between neural circuits, slowing down processing speed and causing working memory deficits (Craig, 2014). It is not surprising, then, that many trauma survivors have deficits with working memory and struggle to recall simple, everyday information (Hollowood, 2018).

Long-term Memory

A second type of neural consolidation process, *system consolidation*, involves the reorganization of engram circuits in response to experience (Dudai, 2004). These neuro-circuits can spread to new locations in the brain while simultaneously diminishing the strength of connections to the hippocampus where they were initially stored. When consolidated memory engrams link with those of other associated circuits, they can speed up consolidation processes by providing a connective network for new information (Tse et al., 2007). Ultimately, trauma survivors' resilience is undergirded by the establishment of positive new neuro-circuits that are linked to the traumatic memories. This example of the brain's capacity to repair itself (also known as *neuroplasticity*) enables survivors to hold their memories of the traumatic events while interrupting the cascade of negative physical and emotional symptoms.

Long-term memory processes are classified into two main types, *declarative* (DM) and *non-declarative* (NDM) (Maslin, 2018c). The hippocampus stores declarative memories. These memory functions are further subdivided into *episodic memory* and *semantic memory* (Maslin, 2018c). Episodic memory processes store memories of experiences and specific events in time, including details of times, places, associated emotions, and other contextual knowledge. They can be explicitly stated and reconstructed. Semantic memories constitute associative learning. They record facts, meanings, concepts, and knowledge about the general factual knowledge shared with others and are independent of personal experience and of the spatial/temporal context in which they were acquired (Maslin, 2018c). Semantic memories are built on episodic memories, but they are more abstract and relational and are associated with the meaning of verbal symbols.

Trauma and declarative memory. Traumatization causes decreased volume in the cerebral cortex and hippocampus (Karl et al., 2006) and decreased hippocampus activity during DM tasks (Shin et al., 2004). Such changes in these areas impair the neuro-circuitry that forms the basis of working memory, executive function, and the regulation of behavior. They are also associated with the emotional deficits associated with PTSD (Simeon et al., 2007).

Further, the cortisol surges caused by traumatic experiences, which result in intense emotional arousal, cause other dysfunctions in the hippocampus. They prevent memories from being processed into neutral narratives (van der Kolk, 1997). Instead, phobias about such memories prevent the integration of traumatic events and split those memories from ordinary consciousness. They then become dissociated fragments of visual images, sensations, and behavioral memories separate from their original episodic neuro-circuits. The dissociative nature of traumatic memories seems to be what distinguishes them from memories of everyday experience. Dissociation at the moment of the trauma now has been established as the single most important predictor for developing PTSD. The flashbacks and nightmares characteristic of PTSD can be seen as products of that dissociation (Shalev, Liberzon, & Marmar, 2017).

Trauma and non-declarative memory. Non-declarative memories (NDM) cannot be brought into awareness with conscious effort (Bauer, 2013). NDM responses are reactionary and unconscious, much like muscle memory. Unlike declarative memory (DM) engrams, they do not involve the hippocampus at all. They are encoded and stored relatively permanently in the areas of the brain which are also involved in motor control (Malin, 2018). NDM are resistant to decay, especially if they are linked to engrams with intense emotional or threat-based content (van der Kolk, 1994). They tap into past experiences – no matter how long ago those experiences occurred – to remember things without thinking about them.

In response to stressful events, a cascade of alarm signals from the sensory organs, especially those of the head and neck, are sent to the part of the hindbrain that is the main source of stress hormones in the cerebral cortex (Bouret & Sara, 2010). This then activates the thalamus and the amygdala. If there is emotional content, the amygdala transmits these signals to the hippocampus that constructs a cognitive context to the information, making them a declarative memory. These memories are then transmitted to the cerebral cortex that mobilizes conscious and autonomic responses to threats.

Fight, Flight or Freeze Responses
When confronted with a perceived threat, the brain and nervous system immediately respond by triggering a series of instinctive physiological survival strategies, summarized in the phrase, "flight, fright, and freeze", also called the acute stress response. These responses, which increase the chances for surviving imminent threats, are trauma-related

examples of NDM in action (Scaer, 2001). During times of acute stress, the brain activates the sympathetic nervous system releasing a surge of stress hormones, noradrenaline and cortisol. These hormones increase cognitive focus and augment oxygenation for muscle movement to prepare for the anticipated fight (LeDoux, 2015). In addition to the brain proper, the autonomic nervous system, specifically the dorsal part of the vagal nerve (Porges, 2001), is hyperactive during fight-or-flight response system and is a major contributor to cardiac and visceral symptoms associated with chronic stress (Vince, 2015).

The fight response is associated with changes in activity levels within the areas of the brain that monitor emotional states. Physiological evidence of the fight response includes: uncontrollable bodily weakness or muscle tenseness, crying, fist clenching, enlarged pupils and darting eyes, flared nostrils, a fixed, tight jaw and teeth grinding, changes in facial expressions, heart palpitations, and sudden sweating accompanied by nausea (Manitoba Trauma Information and Education Centre, n.d.; Shin & Liberzon, 2010).

Traumatization also increases production of other hormones, estrogen and serotonin, which contribute to pain sensitivity. For example, once activated, the brain's sensory neurons signal the adrenal glands to increase stress hormone production, causing constricted blood vessels throughout the body. In turn, this disrupts the body's state of homeostasis and can result in persistent and severe headaches and migraines (American Headache Society, 2016).

The flight response is the adaptation of avoiding perceived threats. Typically, when people perceive situations to be distressing, they feel anxious. When trauma survivors find themselves in situations similar to their original traumatic events, or are reminded of the event, or worry about encountering something similarly threatening, their brains' anterior insular region gets triggered causing the release of noradrenaline and cortisol.

Traumatized people are more prone to panic attacks, an extreme form of anxiety. During a panic attack, a trauma survivor may experience shaky limbs, pins and needles, chest pains, sweating, nausea, migraine headaches, faintness, and a disconnection to her own body. If they go into chronic flight mode, survivors may suffer from shallow breathing, restless feet and legs, and numbness in their extremities. They may also suffer from chronic insomnia or oversleeping.

Prolonged anxiety associated with traumatization can compromise the immune and endocrine systems. Fluctuations in these systems can trigger shingles and other inflammatory conditions. It may cause high blood pressure and high blood sugar which both contribute to immune system suppression. Stressed individuals are also more likely to have bad health habits that put them at greater risk, including poor sleep and nutrition, less exercise, and a greater likelihood of substance abuse (Glaser & Kiecolt-Glaser, 2005).

In the freeze response, the two characteristic psychological traumatic freeze responses, helplessness and hopelessness, are forms of physical shock. They are instinctive reactions to prolonged aversive events that are perceived as uncontrollable and inescapable (Maier & Seligman, 2016). Inescapable threats activate part of the midbrain that processes messages of pain, fear, and anxiety (including distrust) from the nerves in the spinal column that are part of sympathetic nervous system (Porges, 2001). This causes the release of the neurotransmitter serotonin and then activates the amygdala where such painful memories are stored (Behbehani, 1995; Levine, 2012). Typical freeze responses include excessive sweating, dry mouth, and pounding chest or chest pain, decreased or increased heart rate, restricted breathing, bouts of uncontrollable trembling and shaking, feelings of coldness, numbness, skin pallor, and ringing in the ears (Manitoba Trauma Information and Education Centre, n.d.).

Research: Trajectories of Whistleblower Resilience

This chapter is based on findings from one of the author's (Stafford, 2017) dissertation study. Inspired by her own experience as a whistleblower, the study began an as an investigation of the whistleblower-employer-retribution phenomena. Initially, the research question was: *What is the lived experience of public leaders who whistleblow with employer retaliation?* However, as the study progressed, it became clear that the data included important insights on the life restoration process for these particular respondents. Very little research had been done on this aspect of whistleblowing. As a result, after all the interviews were completed, the research question was reframed as an exploratory study to examine this rare occurrence within the broader whistleblower population: *What is the lived experience of public leader whistleblowers who were targets of employer retaliation, and who also experienced posttraumatic growth?*

Although the original study used a mixed-method approach, only the qualitative components are reported here. Archival data provided the contextual evidential documentation, supporting the claim that the organization under study had a politicized culture of corruption. In-depth interview data focused initially on participants' whistleblowing experiences and their biopsychosocial (BPS) impacts over time (Blascovich, Mendes, Tomaka, Salomon, & Seery, 2003).

Applying the Biopsychosocial Model of Challenge and Threat to Whistleblower Resilience

The BPS model is an integrated perspective of health and wellbeing that considers how these individual processes collectively influence behavior when individuals are faced with stressful or threatening conditions (Blascovich et al., 2003). Stafford's application of this theoretical model enabled her to examine factors that bind the biological (physical), the psychological (emotional), and the sociological (family, professional) realities embedded in the public leader whistleblower experience, across a continuum of time.

Participants' achievements of traumatic growth were emergent themes. Posttraumatic growth is conceptualized as positive psychological changes which are experienced as a result of adversity and other challenges that compel some individuals to rise to a higher level of functioning (Tedeschi & Calhoun, 2004). These constitute circumstances that challenge an individual's capacity to adapt and disrupt their way of understanding the world and their place in it. Posttraumatic growth is not about returning to the same life as it was previously experienced before a period of traumatic suffering. Rather, it is about undergoing significant 'life-changing' psychological shifts in thinking and relating to the world that contribute to personal processes of change that are deeply meaningful.

From these findings, Stafford (2017) developed a five-phase, Biopsychosocial (BPS) Trajectory Model. For this chapter, we examine participants' efforts to be resilient as they faced the pain and uncertainties of ongoing employer retaliation during Stages 2 and 3 – prior to reaching their tipping points which launched them into their posttraumatic growth trajectories. (See Figure 2.) Because participants' whistleblower experiences paralleled and validated Stafford's, we have included those in this discussion, too. Stafford's efforts to be resilient are also relevant here because she was able to benefit from newer trauma-informed therapies that the others in her study either didn't have or didn't provide enough details for the authors to know about.

Recruitment. The convenience sample of participants was composed of 11 public agency leaders in County X-U.S. who had been whistleblowers and who had experienced employer retaliation. The sample included 3 men and 8 women, ranging in age from 39 to 50 years. All had been in senior leadership positions before they became whistleblowers. The duration of their employments ranged from one to thirty years. Two had blown the whistle before. The recruitment process and interviews occurred December 2013 through March 2014. Stafford's whistleblowing trauma took place over the last several years she was employed (2001-2012) as the executive director in a public-private partnership organization in County X.

Qualitative data collection. The in-depth, semi-structured interviews were designed to explore the biopsychosocial impacts of the whistleblower-employer retaliation experience before, during, and after the whistleblowing event. The 11 interviews included 12 open-ended questions and ranged in length from 60 to 90 minutes. Since completing her dissertation, Stafford has also engaged in extensive reflections about her trauma narrative and posttrauma recovery process which have been presented at three conferences (Stafford, 2016a, 2016b; Stafford, 2017) and published in two other scholarly publications (Stafford, 2015; Stafford & Meier, 2017).

Findings

Based on her analyses, Stafford created a five-phase model of posttraumatic growth which charts whistleblowers' painful odysseys through traumatization as they sought to fight wrongdoing to the establishment of "new equilibria." Within each phase, she was able to describe the interacting biopsychosocial (BPS) changes these whistleblowers experienced as they tried to cope with the intensifying and diminishing threats. Thus, the BPS dimensions include both negative and positive (e.g., resilient responses) psychological and social impacts. Her graphic, *The Triple Helix: Biopsychosocial Factors in Posttraumatic Growth Trajectory Model* (Figure 2), symbolizes the ways these factors were intertwined in their effects over time. It is an adaption of the Biopsychosocial Model of Challenge and Threat by Blascovich and Tomaka (1996, p.11) and the Posttraumatic Growth Model by Overcash, Calhoun, Cann, and Tedeschi (1996) and Calhoun, Cann, and Tedeschi (2010). The Triple Helix graphic is symbolic of interdependent BPS factors only. It does not represent any specific data.

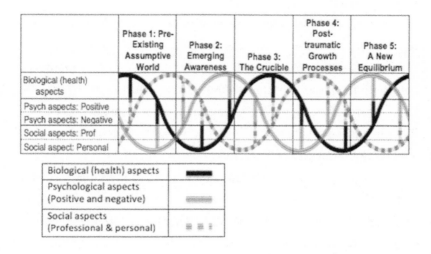

Figure 2. The Triple Helix: Biopsychosocial Factors in Posttraumatic
Growth Trajectory Model.

Here are definitions of the first three phases of the Posttraumatic
Growth Trajectory Model shown in Figure 2.

Phase 1 Theme: Pre-existing assumptive world

Before participants became aware of workplace infractions, their
professional life-worlds felt safe and satisfying. They had good health.
They were able to exercise their leadership authority to achieve their
professional goals and fulfill their organizational missions. Their
personal values were supported through the county's mission statements
and policies and procedures. They were proud to represent their county
to the public. They viewed their roles as servant leaders as a privilege.

Phase II Theme: Emerging awareness

Participants began to sense that something was amiss in in their organizations when they became aware that legal or moral improprieties
had occurred. As they began to recruit resources (trustworthy allies,
information, advice, knowledge and skills), their efforts confirmed that
the initial "challenge of corruption" was an actual threat.

Phase III Theme: "The Crucible"

Participants' lived experiences of employer retaliation after they reported confirmed infractions through their organizations' chains of command, or external authorities, spurred their desperate attempts to cope with mounting workplace conflict and chaos. Perpetrators and their subordinates stigmatized, marginalized, and threatened them. Participants' core values and beliefs were called into question. All aspects of their lives were scarred.

For this chapter, we focus on Phase II (Emerging Awareness) and Phase III (The Crucible) which posed increasing challenges to these whistleblowers' resilience. The Phase III descriptor, The Crucible, refers to a stage in the metaphorical "Hero's Journey" in which the hero, after feeling called to step off her conventional life path, is forced to endure many trials and tribulations through which she acquires skills, resources, allies, and ultimately new perspectives on life (Campbell, 2008; Lawson, 2005). In the next section, we will summarize: 1) how symptoms of traumatization began to manifest in participants' biological, psychological, and social systems, 2) the resilience strategies they used in their efforts to regain "normality" that characterized Phase I, and 3) examples of the outcomes of those efforts.

Biological Impacts of Trauma

Stafford and her study participants experienced many stress-related biological symptoms that interfered significantly with their intimate relations, work, and social activities. These are presented below. All names (except for Stafford) are participants' pseudonyms.

Physical Indicators of Psychological Trauma

Robert: I had stress-related diverticulitis. It attacks you in your intestines and causes an incredible amount of pain.

Cleo: I got shingles. I didn't know what they were. I'd never had them before. The pain became excruciating.

Aliciah: I would come home every night with a throbbing migraine, to the point of vomiting. I would have to take my migraine medication and go to sleep right away.

Effie: I had to start taking high blood pressure medicine (for the first time) …I also started having muscle spasms and had to take muscle relaxants…I lost a lot of weight – about 30 lbs. And then my hair started falling out and I started having acne problems.

Interference with Family Relationships

Sarah: My marriage was suffering because I was so tired when I got home, I wasn't, you know, very friendly. I was always sort of withdrawn. I started becoming very withdrawn from my family. So, this particular issue did cause a lot of friction in my marriage.

Aliciah: I wouldn't tell my parents everything because their older; I didn't want to work them…When I did visit them and happened to mention here and there what was happening, my dad would "be a dad" and get all irate. He would tell me, "You need to leave that job."

K-Pax: During those peak periods, it put stress on my family and they would let me know about it. I'd come home angry, and if I decided to do the less healthy route and have a cigar or drink, they'd say, "Why are you doing that? It's not good for you." At one point, I had such bad moods my family couldn't stand to be around me. They'd yell at me, "Knock that shit off! You've got to stop!" Yeah, they did get tough on me.

Seeking Medical treatments for Stress-Related Health Problems

Cleo: The pain became so excruciating that I forced myself to go to the doctor, because nothing else was working. The doctor took one look at me and said, "You need to take a few weeks off."

Aliciah: I kept thinking, "It can't get worse." But that only works for so long and then you just have to face reality. That's when I thought, "I do need to go on medical leave of absence because what I am experiencing is just not healthy."

Liz: I went to the doctor because I was having trouble sleeping. He told me my insomnia was stress-related, and so were my problems with high blood pressure and high blood sugar levels.

Participants' symptoms were severe enough to spur them to seek medical attention. Stafford and three others were forced to take medical leaves. Stafford and all her study participants were diagnosed with stress-related psychological disorders, although, except for Stafford who was diagnosed with PTSD, they did not specify their diagnoses in their interview. Seven were also prescribed psychiatric medications to deal with their emotional distress. Seven (including Stafford) sought psychotherapy. Two others reported that they had not gone for therapy but, in retrospect, wished they had.

Impact of Resilience Strategies

Over time, as they continued to implement their resilience strategies, participants' physical stress symptoms diminished and their sense of wellbeing increased. They used fewer health care services and medications while also engaging in more self-care activities. Here are the resilience indicators they reported.

Symptoms of Physical and Psychological Stress Diminish or Disappear

Liz: Six months after leaving my job, my doctor redid my blood work. My blood sugar levels and hormones were all completely normal. I was really surprised that getting rid of all my job stress made that much of a difference.

Sabrina: After leaving my job, I had a lot less anxiety. *A lot*! Now I have a lot less issues with my stomach. I feel a lot more relaxed. I was so relieved because the situation at work was so toxic for me personally. I think my health generally is so much better now.

Increased Tolerance for Physiological Arousal

Abby: I realized over time that I physically [let go of the negativity] when I was driving home up the mountain. And I would take my time and, sometimes, I listened to music or roll down the window and listen to the birds. It has truly been a magical thing, being able to live up here and let all that stress go.... Who needs meds when you have these mountains surrounding you?

Emerson: It's kind of like a scar. If there's a way I can avoid going into stressful situations, I will. I'm not always able to. That's a lasting impact because it still hurts to remember. I think part of coping is, you know, pushing things out of your mind and not thinking about them. Perhaps, that's not the best coping mechanism, but it's a "man thing." Why should I subject myself to all those bad memories? It's just easier to try to avoid all those situations.

Decreased or Discontinued Medication Use for Stress-Related Conditions

Participants' stress-related health problems that no longer required medication included: diabetes, high blood pressure, high cholesterol, chronic pain, appetite disorders, insomnia, migraine headaches, and shingles.

Increased Self-care Activities to Regain Physical Wellbeing

Effie: Once when things were really bad, a friend picked me up and took me to get a massage. And she paid for everything! They gave me a facial and a body massage, and they gave me some chamomile tea. And it was one of the most relaxing things that I had ever had in my life, to that point. I went to sleep and I woke up feeling just like a new person. Oh, it was wonderful!

Sunshine: When I got stressed out, I'd go for a long walk. It helped to change my breathing pattern. So, if I was feeling pressure in my chest,

73

like I was going to have an anxiety attack, then I'd go for a little walk around the building. Sometimes I'd go for a walk at night when I got home, and that seemed to help.

Psychological Impacts of Trauma

Adult traumatization can be complicated by traumatic events that occurred in childhood. These early experiences are embodied as associative neural networks connecting and interacting with many parts of the brain, and they influence how new information is processed (Gilboa & Marlatte, 2017.) These networks are expressed behaviorally as cognitive "schemas." They are stable and enduring patterns, comprising of memories, bodily sensations, emotions, and cognitions. These stable belief systems function as rules that govern information processing and behavior. Often operating at the unconscious level, they inform the individual's interpretation of contexts and events and enable rapid, often automatic coping responses. Challenges to schemas can be very threatening and activate intense physical reactions and feelings.

Schemas drive adaptive or maladaptive coping strategies (Beck et al., 1990). Individuals can have multiple interacting schemas. Adaptive schemas are reality based and congruent with goal attainment. Maladaptive schemas are associated with persistent cognitive biases and dysfunctional consequences – emotional distress, and self-defeating or self-harming behaviors. Adults who have experienced interpersonal traumas in their younger years are more likely to show maladaptive schemas as adults (Karatzias, Jowett, Begley, & Deas, 2016). In complex traumatization, maladaptive schemas stemming from traumas in earlier life can be reactivated when current challenges arise which resonate with those earlier traumas and which then interfere with survivors' capacities to cope effectively. Here is how Stafford describes the experience of retriggering her whistleblower trauma-based maladaptive schema.

Stafford: While working on an article about secondary traumatization which was based on my experiences doing doctoral research (Stafford & Meier, 2017), I had to review the interview the interviews of my participants' traumas. As I traced back how doing the research had affected me I was stunned at the way my traumatization was retriggered. I vividly recalled my own experience of being called into a meeting where my boss reamed me out for going on medical leave. She screamed and yelled at me in front of my new supervisor. I felt deeply humiliated and betrayed because I had believed that she had my back and that I could count on her support through the whistleblowing process. I remember feeling helpless, trembling and nauseated. I had flashbacks, insomnia and nightmares the entire time I was working on the article.

Psychological Aspects of the Fight, Flight or Freeze Response

Each one of the body's instinctual responses to threat are coupled with feelings and cognitions that are the brain's meaning making processes. Fight and flight responses are stimulated by spikes in adrenaline which prepare the body to confront a threat or flee from it. When it seems like neither escape or avoidance is possible, the dorsal raphe nucleus on the midline of the brain stem is activated evoking the freeze response. These changes in the brain and nervous system are expressed as major psychological symptoms: intrusive thoughts, avoidance, negative cognitions and moods, and excessive arousal and reactivity.

Behavior: Intrusive Thoughts

Trauma symptoms: Nightmares, unwanted thoughts about traumatic events, flashbacks, reacting to traumatic reminders with intense distress or physiological reactivity

Behavior: Avoidance

Trauma symptoms: Avoiding triggers for traumatic memories, including places, conversations, and other reminders

Behavior: Negative Alterations in Cognition and Moods

Trauma symptoms: Distorted blame of self or others for traumatic events, negative beliefs about oneself or the world, persistent negative emotions such as fear, guilt, shame, feeling alienated, and constricted affect (e.g. inability to experience positive emotions)

Behavior: Alterations in Arousal and Reactivity (Emotional Dysregulation)

Trauma symptoms: Angry, reckless, or self-destructive behavior, sleep problems, concentration problems, increased startle responses, and hypervigilance

As documented below, Stafford and her study participants experienced many or all of these debilitating symptoms as they progressed through the Crucible stage. Stafford and study participants were all ultimately diagnosed with TSRD/PTSD.

Intrusive Thoughts

Cleo: It's like you go under, under the water. And you are only able to come up for a few moments and look around to get your bearings. And then, you're sucked back in because information is coming. And it's in your mind, and you're thinking all the time about that there were real threats.

Hyper-Arousal and Hyper-Reactivity

Robert: I'm sure I used bad language…and I know I drank [a lot] at those venting sessions. And, I would kind of lose it at different times.

Emerson: I felt angry and a deep sense of sadness. Even as a grown man, I mean. I was fighting back the tears, you know. I thought, "This is just grossly unfair." (His voice cracks as he fights back tears.) I didn't do anything wrong. So, I was feeling both the anger and the hurt.

Avoidance

Effie: It was awful. I didn't know who to trust. I could not trust anyone at work. I didn't know if people who were nice to me were just being nice because they wanted to get close to me to set me up. It was really bad. I ate lunch alone. I didn't really joke or talk to anyone because I didn't know how they would take it, or what they would say and just take what I said and twist it. So, those last six months were very lonely, and very dysfunctional for me.

Robert: At times, you're utterly depressed because of what was happening. On the weekends, you go home and you fret. You worry about how you are going to take care of your family, what your next move is, and how you can get out of the situation. That's all you think about.

Negative Changes in Cognitions and Moods

Liz: It was very disheartening and depressing. To have this happen at this point in my life. I just never expected it. I never saw it coming.

Psychological Resilience Strategies

Resourceful people have many adaptive schemas they can draw on to manage or overcome challenges. Stafford and whistleblowers in her study were all high functioning professionals. As they started to implement their various resilience strategies, they were able to reactivate their adaptive schemas or learn new ones. Some were instinctive, serendipitous, or the result of therapy. With the help of their therapists and their own dogged efforts to rebuild their lives, these whistleblowers learned to apply stress management and problem-focused coping strategies that helped them to grieve, to come to terms with their losses, and to claim their identities as trauma survivors instead of victims. Among other things, this involved shifting to adaptive cognitive schemas that enabled them to let go of their feelings of shame and self-blame. They began to experience more a positive sense of self-worth and a renewed life purpose that reaffirmed their positive core values. Here are examples of the resilience strategies they used to achieve these outcomes.

Adaptive Cognitive Schemas

Sunshine: It was just enough to know I was making a difference. Even though that difference is small, but at least I was trying.

Robert: I thought to myself, "What is the best I can do? If I run this system as well as I can, I'm helping 30,000 county employees make sure they're taken care of. That's almost 95 percent, all of whom deserve it. That's a great thing. And then you have the 5 percent who are corrupt, doing wrong thing. I'll try to fight those where I can but knowing what I did for all those others who worked their whole careers, and that's all they had. That was enough for me to keep fighting.

Cleo: Ultimately, I trusted history, that time would overcome everything as it has in the past. And yet, if you read history, the bleak present passes and a new beginning is around the corner. The drill is to stand in the storm and to hang on, so that when it is over and things do start over, you're there. That was a big reason not to give up.

Emotional Coping

Abby: I took it extremely, extremely hard. So I wrote a long letter to a person who was part of the larger organization telling her what was going on. She was somebody who had trained me in my job. I really respected her and this was the basis that spurred me to blow the whistle. I got a letter back from her saying, "There's a book you need to read, it's called Co-dependent No More." And I thought, "Oh my gosh, is that what this is about? *Am I trying to fix something that I shouldn't be trying to fix?*"

Problem-Focused Coping

Aliciah: Well, honestly, I know that people say when you start talking to yourself, you know you're really crazy [laughing]. For a while there, I guess it was true! But, seriously, that was one of the things that kept me sane – especially the unbearable days. I literally had to brainwash myself *every morning*. I had to remind myself, "This is just a job, it is not your whole life." *Every morning,* I would sigh and tell myself, "Ok. Clock in. Clock out. You can do this."

Robert: It was damned if you do, damned if you don't. A no win scenario. So, I found a whole new way to deal with the stress. I would go to the gym and workout as hard as I could to burn through all the stress. I was just trying to stay positive, but it was an unbelievable battle.

Letting Go of Shame, Victimization, and Self-Blame

Liz: I was in Hawaii what I had one of those ah-ha moments. I thought, "You've been doing this for 32 years, you don't need to take this crap. You've got other options." And I really thought that there would be nothing for me outside of that job. And that is crazy thinking. There are always options, there are always thing you can do. Life does not end because you end a career. You just move on to a different career.

Sarah: After I blew the whistle, I stayed with my job. But what I love about my job now is that I do have autonomy now. For example, in planning the third anniversary of the program, I don't want a bunch of "politicals" to talk about how great they're doing here. I want to let my kids talk. And I have the autonomy and authority to make this happen—my way, not "theirs."

K-Pax: I recently retired from a position that I really enjoyed. But I am still very active on a number of non-profit boards. I am doing some consulting with the League of Cities. So, professionally, I'm still very much engaged, although it's nice to have more freedom than I've had in the past.

Regaining a Sense of Self-Worth and Life Purpose

Sabrina: My work psychology has definitely improved with my new job. I have a lot more confidence. I feel like I could step in and do any other job. When I left my old job, I didn't feel that way.

Sarah: When the Director of Human Services asked whether I would take back my resignation. I said, "No. You mistreated my executive director who was doing everything right and he stood up to the [corrupt] Board of Supervisors. I respect that. I don't respect you guys. However, I will charge you a $150 an hour if you'd like me to stay here for another month as a consultant." And they paid up!

Sarah, again: I once saw a quote, "You should only work to live, not live to work." My colleagues and I talked a lot about that. I told them, "You know what, this is a job. It's not my life. And although the work ethic is a big thing for me. My family is more important. The only reason I work is to have enough money to live."

Social Impacts of Trauma

Whistleblowers in this study reported both professional and personal tribulations also found in other whistleblower studies (Bjorkelo, 2013; Mesmer-Magnus & Viswesvaran, 2005). At work, they were targets of repeated bullying. Formal reprisals from superiors took the form of loss of leadership authority, demotions, transfers, and reprimands. Unofficial reprisals included: the disregard of their concerns, exclusion from key meetings, character shaming, threats, ostracism, and pressures to resign. Stafford and all of her informants commented frequently about their growing distrust of their colleagues, leaders, and administrations. It was impossible to know who among their coworkers they could trust, leaving them feeling increasingly isolated and helpless. Their organizations' whistleblower protection policies and procedures were not followed; they were betrayed by their institutions and unable to fight back. Here are examples of the social impacts on whistleblowers as professionals.

Professional Impacts

Effie: I didn't think [blowing the whistle] would cost me my job. I ended up being interviewed for a field rep position. I took it thinking I could get away from it all by going there. But by leaving the other organization and now going to another County X office, the harassment just followed me there. They started picking on me there immediately. If I was two minutes late, a supervisor would comment that I was late that day. And, if I went to lunch, I was scrutinized. I couldn't be a minute late getting back. They would pick on me about stuff like if I went to someone and said, "Hi." In the beginning it was little things that just got really bad.

Robert: It was definitely retaliation...Not only were they attacking me and sending people to meetings who had never been there before. They were *meant* to be threatening, get involved, and to put pressure on the appointed board members. Those members who wouldn't go along were removed from their positions. The new members who replaced them all started to put pressure on the program, threatening to dismantle it. It was always verbal. Because they didn't want to put anything on paper, nobody put anything in writing.

Emerson: It felt like my hands were tied. Maybe calling it a sense of paranoia is not too strong, because it was born out later. I wasn't paranoid about anything in particular. But I was beginning to be fearful when I had to take a step or make a decision. I felt like I was being second-guessed at almost every turn.

Family and Non-Work Impacts

Damage to whistleblowers' social relationships extends beyond the work place. The impact is systemic (Klarik, Kvesic, Mandic, Petrov, & Franciskovic, 2013). Family lives are "hijacked" (Smith, n.d.). The trauma victim's distress can be transferred to people in their immediate surroundings, with symptoms similar to those of PTSD (secondary traumatization). For Stafford and her informants, emotional numbing (freeze responses) and the need to protect family members from their fears often inhibited them from reaching out, carrying out normal household responsibilities, and functioning socially outside their homes. Trauma survivors can have diminished sexual drive and problems of sexual functioning. Hypervigilance, including increased irritability, could result in outbursts of anger, rage, and hostility. Seven of the study participants reported that their marriages were severely strained by the consequences of their whistleblowing. One was divorced as a result.

Robert: I went to parties and drank like one beer. But I could never relax and I would never stay very long. When I met a new person I would think, "There's nothing wrong with this guy. I don't know him at all. He's probably trustworthy, right? He probably doesn't even know the people I deal with." But at that point, I didn't trust anyone. And the last thing I wanted to do is have four beers in me and start slipping up and say something that would get me in trouble. So, I changed my social behavior. I changed my approach to my friends. I started clamping down. And it was all because of distrust and fear. *Flat out fear*.

Often the act of whistleblowing can be even more traumatic when it results in sudden job losses along with loss of benefits (Kline, 2014). It is a testimony to all eleven of the participants' resilience, that they were all able to continue working. Nine found new jobs, two kept their same jobs. Stafford retired with disability and continued on to complete a doctoral program. Her dissertation research, the basis of this chapter, was inspired by her whistleblower experience.

Resilience Strategies

Resilience from traumatization's social impacts involves multiple dimensions. Survivors must work to gradually rebuild their sense of internal and external safety. They must reclaim the ability to trust with family and friends and determine who else in their social networks is trustworthy. As their nervous systems calm and they are better able to focus, they can resume their family responsibilities and reengage with work. Here are examples of how participants were able to establish the basis for a new, healthy equilibrium through social support.

Effie: But the people that knew me, knew better. And they stood by my side. The people in my church stood by me. . . And, actually, the community came out for me. There was a huge community meeting, over three hundred people were there. There was a big press conference and they supported me in this.

Aliciah: I am glad to have family and friends that talked to me and just walked me through the whole process. And, you know, I was able to just work through it. I had a lot of support which was a blessing. It truly was.

Abby: I've gone back to my old personality, where I just enjoy being around people. I've joined a quilters club. I do sewing and I do philanthropic stuff. So, I'm making the best of what I have now.

Therapeutic Resources to Promote Whistleblower Resilience
Pharmacological Treatments for Trauma Symptoms

Stafford and her study participants were all coping with their traumatic experiences in the period between 2005 and 2011. During that time, there were relatively fewer choices in therapies to alleviate their emotional distress. Cognitive behavior therapy and psychotropic medications for anxiety and depression were the treatments of choice. Medications were, and still are, used to alleviate four trauma-related symptom clusters characteristic of the PTSD diagnosis: intrusive thoughts, avoidance, negative cognitions and moods, and alterations in arousal and reactivity (Jeffreys, 2017).

Most traumatized patients receive some kind of pharmacological treatment, including antidepressant agents (89%) anxiolytic or sedative-hypnotic agents (61%), anxiolytic or sedative–hypnotic agents, and antipsychotic agents (34%) (Shalev, Liberzon, & Marmar, 2017). Medications prescribed for treating trauma symptoms broadly act upon neurotransmitters affecting the fear and anxiety circuitry (serotonin and noradrenaline) of the brain (Jeffreys, 2017). Studies show that the types of medications listed above are helpful in minimizing trauma symptoms, but they have the disadvantage of taking a month or more to become fully effective (Chedekel, 2012). Further, most of the time, they provide symptom reduction but do not extinguish symptoms entirely (Jeffreys, 2017).

Depression is nearly three to five times more likely in those with psychological trauma than those without such traumas (Kessler, 1995). It is not surprising, then, that the most studied medications for treating PTSD are antidepressants, which may help control trauma symptoms such as sadness, worry, anger, and feeling emotionally numb (National Institute of Mental Health, 2016). The Federal Drug Administration (FDA) has approved four antidepressants that have the strongest evidence of their effectiveness. Three are specific serotonin reuptake inhibitors (SSRIs) that are widely known by their brand names: Zoloft, Paxil, and Prozac. The FDA has also approved, Effexor, a serotonin norepinephrine inhibitor, but all four these are only moderately effective (Shalev et al., 2017). To reduce risk of relapse, patients must receive a full therapeutic dose for 6 to 12 months. Used alone, these agents alleviate symptoms but rarely reduce risk of remission. There is substantial risk of relapse once these medications are discontinued.

Other medications have appeared to be promising for PTSD treatments, but they have not been approved by the Food and Drug Administration (e.g., are "off label"). The evidence supporting their use is weak (Jeffreys, 2017). This may be because the particular medication has not been widely tested in populations with PTSD, or it has not been shown to be effective. The 2017 Veterans Administration Clinical Practice Guideline for PTSD only supports the uses of these medications when the four strongly recommended medications listed above are ineffective, unavailable, or not tolerated (Department of Veterans Affairs, 2017).

Despite the fact that pharmacological treatments are commonly used to treat psychological symptoms of trauma, trauma-focused psychotherapies have been found to be more efficacious than pharmacotherapy and are strongly recommended treatments. In the few studies that have provided comparisons of two evidence-based therapies, cognitive behavioral therapies and EMDR (Eye Movement Desensitization and Reprocessing), show greater effect sizes than antidepressants. While some patients prefer medication to psychotherapy, research indicates that, when given the choice, a majority choose psychotherapy (Simiola, Neilson, Thompson, & Cook, 2015). Based upon current knowledge, most prescribing clinicians view pharmacotherapy more as an important adjunct to the evidenced-based psychotherapies for PTSD rather than a sole treatment strategy.

Trauma-Informed Psychotherapies
Neuroscience has contributed to our knowledge about the balanced function of the autonomic nervous system's (ANS) sympathetic and parasympathetic branches. When the ANS is in a healthy balance, we have access to a conscious system of information processing in which stress chemicals do not block access to the cerebral cortex. This condition enables problem-solving and strategic thinking in stressful situations rather than reactivity, as well as the ability to engage in pro-social behaviors (Roozendaal, McEwen, & Chattarji, 2009).

These advances provide the context for the discussion that follows on five models of trauma informed psychotherapy that are currently in use. These include: conventional Cognitive Behavioral Therapies (CBT) and neuro-science informed Cognitive Behavioral Therapies (n-CBT), Eye Movement Desensitization and Reprocessing, Coherence Therapy, and Energy Psychology (EP)-based therapies. As an optimistic finale, we offer a brief overview of their processes and potential benefits for promoting whistle blower resilience. Readers who want more detailed information about specific therapeutic processes can find links to authoritative websites in the Appendix.

Those study participants who had psychotherapy received CBT and antidepressants. Stafford was the only one who received n-CBT treatment and antidepressants. While she was working on her dissertation, she worked with a coach (co-author Meier) who used a form of Energy Psychology-based therapy to help her deal successfully with the predictable stress of dissertation research, including re-traumatization evoked by interviewing and analyzing her informants' data (Stafford, 2016b; Stafford & Meier, 2017).

Conventional Cognitive Behavioral Therapy. Conventional CBT is best defined as "a group of therapeutic approaches that share the common premise that thoughts, beliefs, and cognitions cause emotional and behavioral experiences rather than external events" (Field, Beeson, & Jones, 2015, p. 207). CBT theory attributes dysfunctional emotional and behavior responses to dysfunctional thinking (e.g., maladaptive schemas). Based on these assumptions, treatment strategies focus on "confronting, disputing, and restructuring maladaptive thought patterns into more adaptive ones that can lead to more adaptive emotional and behavioral responses" (Field et al., 2015, p. 207).

What happens in conventional CBT sessions? CBT-based counseling aims to modify the clients' irrational beliefs, thereby preventing emotional distress or dysfunctional behaviors (Field et al., 2015). CBT employs an educational model in which the therapist engages in a gentle inquiry process to help patients evaluate and respond to their automatic thoughts and beliefs (e.g., their maladaptive cognitive schemas). CBT therapeutic approaches help clients reduce their distressing arousal levels (amygdala hyperactivity) by teaching them skills (increasing cerebral cortex activity) to identify and evaluate their "automatic thoughts" and to correct their thinking and problem-solving strategies so they are more closely aligned to reality and better serve their life goals (Beck Institute for Cognitive Behavior Therapy, n.d.).

In the case of traumatized clients, therapists may also incorporate exposure-based psychotherapeutic approaches (What Is Exposure Therapy? n.d.). In exposure-oriented sessions, clients recount their traumatic experiences to the therapist in brief chunks, making it easier to learn to tolerate their intense emotions as they gradually process and become desensitized to their vivid memories.

CBT has been widely used to research the effects of psychotherapy for a range of psychiatric problems because the method is standardized. A meta-analysis of CBT used to treat a wide variety of disorders, including PTSD and others that are co-morbid with CBT, documents how this therapy can normalize pre-treatment hypoactivity in the frontal cortex and suppress activity levels in the amygdala (Barsaglini, Sartori, Benetti, Pettersson-Yeo, & Mechelli, 2013).

n-Cognitive Behavioral Therapies. While recent variants of CBT introduced in the past two decades now place less emphasis on the centrality of thought as the cause of emotional distress (Becker & Zayfert, 2001; Hayes, Luoma, Bond, Masuda, & Lillis, 2006), the central focus of the CBT paradigms still envisions all mental disorders in terms of their underlying cognitions and schemas (Beck & Haigh, 2014). They now incorporate mindfulness meditation and other mind-body approaches to suppress amygdala and dorsal vagal hyperactivity and CBT techniques to increase activity in the frontal lobes. For example, in 2015, Field and his colleagues proposed a new conceptual model of neuroscience-informed CBT (n-CBT). It, too, assumes that internal and external stimuli interact to produce emotions, behaviors, and thoughts. However, the model also integrates new knowledge from neuroscience (Porges, n.d.) and interpersonal neurobiology (Siegel, 2012).

The clinical goals of n-CBT are identical to conventional CBT—

to help clients to respond differently to antecedents and to develop more regulated emotional states and functional behavioral responses (Field et al., 2015). n-CBT differs from conventional CBT because it emphasizes client education in the ways their brains and nervous systems respond to stressful events. This kind of psychoeducation about neuroplasticity can reignite clients' hope and a sense of empowerment that life restoration is possible (Field et al., 2015; Siegel, 2010).

What happens in n-CBT sessions? In early stages of n-CBT, clients learn techniques to avoid sending arousal messages to the cerebral cortex and to calm their vagal responses (fight, flight, or freeze). This enables them to come to terms emotionally with what happened to them. They also use mindfulness, biofeedback, neuro-feedback, healthy coping behaviors that activate the senses, and techniques that help them tolerate their physiological and emotional responses. By making it safe to experience their bodily sensations and desire to react, clients' frontal lobes can process new sensory input in order to evaluate, critique, problem-solve, and plan for a response. These changes offer clients opportunities to reappraise their feelings and behaviors and the thoughts that subsequently arise.

Clients are coached to use systematic incremental desensitization, experimenting to see whether and how much their arousal responses diminish in intensity in situations that had previously evoked anxiety and fear. Along with increasing self-acceptance, clients learn how to use positive self-talk to feel safer, focusing on their capacity to be at ease in those settings. They practice discerning whether and how differences in the situation lower their chances of being re-traumatized, as well as recalling memories of their successful efforts to act normally in similar situations.

Eye Movement Desensitization and Reprocessing (EMDR) Therapy. EMDR therapy is an integrative, exposure-based

88

psychotherapy approach (Center for Substance Abuse Treatment, 2014). It bridges the spectrum of trauma-informed treatments from CBT to more mind-body approaches. Introduced by Francis Shapiro in 1992, it has been consistently proven effective for the treatment of trauma (Shapiro, 2002). The protocol incorporates elements from many different treatment approaches, including CBT, exposure therapy, and mindfulness. Each EMDR session is highly structured, including repeated standardized assessments of changes in distress levels and positive cognitions (Maxfield & Solomon, n.d.). As with CBT, a review of research on the benefits of EMDR found evidence that levels of neurological activity changed differentially across various areas of the brain. EMDR also appears to enhance the functional balance between the limbic areas (amygdala and hippocampus) and the cerebral cortex areas which control the emotions.

What happens in EMDR sessions? Sessions begin with training the client in self-care techniques (to enable her to tolerate strong emotions) and brief re-exposure to a "target" cognition about a traumatizing situation. Targets can include past memories, current triggering situations, and future goals. Once a client identifies a target, the therapist uses CBT approaches to help the client identify negative ("irrational") beliefs about it. The therapist also coaches the client in the use of mindfulness techniques to enable her to tolerate re-experiencing the traumatizing cognition ("I'm helpless...") vividly, including awareness of associated body sensations. The therapist then leads the client through a desensitization process using simple motor tasks (typically, side-to-side eye movements, following the therapist's finger). These motor exercises are repeated until the client reports no more emotional distress about the target cognition using the standardize rating scale. Then the therapist asks the client to think of a "preferred" positive belief ("I have the power to ...") related to the target cognition and to focus on this belief while continuing with the motor exercise. The exercise ends when the client reports feeling confident and comfortable, with a positive sense of self when recalling the target cognition and planning for how to cope with other events that might trigger distress and generation of positive images and strategies for resourceful coping.

Applying Neuroplasticity to Promote Emotional Resilience

Neuroplasticity refers to the brain's capacity to change its cellular structures and inter-cellular processes in response to experience. Both CBT and n-CBT use the experience of counteractive thoughts to extinguish distressing memories, and to enhance the emotional self-regulation (Ecker, Ticic, & Hulley, 2012). In the case of n-CBT, clients engage their frontal lobes as they learn to tolerate physiological arousal and reappraise to stress-related memories simply as arousal instead of threat signals. Unfortunately, these changes take a long time to achieve and effort to sustain. Unwanted implicit memory circuits remain fully intact, so traumatized clients remain vulnerable to having old memories flair up again if they find themselves in settings that spark traumatic associations.

Memory Reconsolidation

In 1997, neuroscientists discovered the phenomenon of memory *reconsolidation* which deploys the brain's ability to re-access previously-encoded information about events or information from the past. The strength of network pathways determines how quickly a memory can be recalled. The brain reactivates neural networks originally established in response to a particular event, echoing the brain 's perception of the real event (McLeod, 2007). However, the neuro-circuitry involved in retrieval of a memory is not quite identical to the original encoding, but is linked to associated memories, awareness of current situations, other novel stimuli and distant neural networks (Maslin, 2018b). If trauma survivors' engrams of the factual, sensory and emotional aspects (semantic memory) of their traumatic experiences are disrupted in the hippocampus, survivors' risk of developing PTSD later increases.

Trauma survivors' mental narratives of their traumatic experiences can be coherent, or broken and incoherent. Coherent narratives are "temporally sequenced, detailed, coherent and embedded with personal meaning" (Tuval-Mashiach et al., 2004, p.291). Survivors who later develop PTSD symptoms, tend to have narratives which lack these key characteristics. Many survivors also have "consistent, circumscribed, and stable memory gaps that are limited to brief moments on the most horrifying moments of the insult or assault." Such moments of amnesia are often intermingled with feelings of survivor guilt (Yovell, Bannett, & Shalev, 2003, p.264).

When a neural network returns a memory from long-term storage to short-term memory, it is accessed as kind of mirror image of the initial encoding process (Maslin, 2018a). Typically, the network is then re-stored back in long-term memory, thus re-consolidating and strengthening it. This neuroplastic process is called reconsolidation. The process of reconsolidation may, however, change the original network by linking it to other networks (emotions, current sensory stimuli or subsequently acquired knowledge). This process, in turn may change meanings and expectations which are also incorporated into the network content. Coherence and energy psychology approaches to trauma therapy, described below, utilize these neural mechanisms to erase traumatic memories.

Coherence Therapy. Following the discovery of memory consolidation, Ecker and his colleagues were able to apply the principles of memory deconsolidation and reconsolidation to develop a psychotherapeutic protocol which he named Coherence Therapy (CT) (Ecker et al., 2012). The goal of this approach is to achieve coherence of the emotional brain, the subcortical regions, and the right brain. The aim is to "move the coherence that is intrinsic to implicit emotional memories and bring them into conscious awareness, creating new autobiographical coherence most meaningfully and authentically" (Ecker, Ticic, & Hulley, 2013, p.95).

What happens in Coherence Therapy sessions? As with the two CBT therapies and EMDR, the initial stages of CT work involve a multistep process of vivid re-experiencing which constitutes the far greater part of the therapeutic work. The tasks of this phase are designed "to bring to light key areas of the client's complex, rich, and tender inner worlds" (Ecker, 2011). First, the client describes the specific behaviors, emotions, and thoughts associated with the problem that brings her into therapy. The therapist helps the client bring into awareness the implicit emotional learning(s) (maladaptive schemas) that underlie and drive the presenting problem. The client recalls a vivid positive experience that is incompatible (e.g., "They cannot both be true.") with her symptoms.

The therapist then works with the client to work through three more stages to complete the erasure of symptom-related emotional learnings. Typically, the process can be done quickly. First, the client is asked to reactivate the target emotional learning and to experience strongly the emotions and the somatic sensations associated with it. Second, the client is coached to experience something that contradicts the target learning. This unlocks the synapses of the target emotional learning. Such concurrent contradictory experiences are mismatches from what the reactivated target memory "expects." This evokes an experience of "edgy, experiential dissonance" and the thought that "both cannot possibly be true, yet both feel true" (Ecker, 2011). In the final stage, this process is repeated several times, with the contradictory learning serving as new learning that "disconfirms the original target learning and rewrites the memory circuits so the original emotional learning no longer exists. This shift is experienced as "a deep unlearning and profound release, felt bodily, of the emotional grip of the original learning" (Ecker, 2011).

While still unlocked, these memories can be altered (reconsolidated) by a positive new learning if it occurs within five or six hours following a session. After that, the neural circuits of the altered learning are again locked (reconsolidated) into a stable state (Ecker, 2011). An additional benefit is that only the specific, targeted emotional response is affected, with no loss of corresponding factual or autobiographical memory. Coherence therapy has been found to be effective in eliminating symptoms of PTSD and other co-morbid anxiety and mood disorders (Ecker et al., 2012). What is more impressive is that the positive changes can be sustained effortlessly over the long term (What Is Coherence Therapy? n.d.).

Energy Psychology-based Psychotherapies. Energy psychology (EP)-based therapies also deploy the transformative potential of neuroplasticity to change longstanding patterns in the brain. For example, Emotional Freedom Techniques (EFT), one most widely used EP methods, uses manual stimulation of the acupressure points (referred to as "accupoints" from here on) by tapping, holding, or massaging specific points in a specific sequence. EP protocols pair psychological exposure with accupoint stimulation. Cortisol causes fragmentation of emotional memories in the amygdala making it difficult to recall vividly all the aspects of a focal traumatic event. Further, over time, associations and negative beliefs associated with traumatic events and their repercussions may also resonate in memory and retrigger distress.

What happens in an EFT session? As in CT, clients learn to tolerate recalling anxiety-inducing memories. The important difference with EFT and CT is the use of tapping on specific accupoints. For treatments involving participants with PTSD, exposure typically involves using words or imagery to trigger a traumatic memory. Applying cognitive restructuring principles, clients then repeat self-acceptance statements as they activate the prescribed accupoints. Before and after each round, they self-rate their level of distress. Usually, distress level ratings diminish after each round. The process is repeated until clients' ratings of distress have decreased--ideally to one or zero (Church & Feinstein, 2013). Depending on the complexity and severity of the focal trauma, several sessions may be needed to clear event-specific and associated aspects of a traumatizing experience (Davidson & Sherod, 2013).

EP therapies have shown lasting benefits in alleviating other psychiatric conditions that are often comorbid with PTSD, including: specific phobias, specific anxieties, generalized anxiety, depression, physical pain, and chronic illnesses. Studies of EP treatments found that they effectively alleviated trauma symptoms on an average of fewer than five sessions (Feinstein, 2010).

Benefits of EFT. Once trauma and related symptoms are alleviated, EP techniques can support resilience. Modified EFT protocols have been developed to empower clients and promote "peak performance" (Church, 2014). Clients easily learn to do EFT themselves when faced with situations which evoke feelings of low self-confidence or low self-worth. They can act quickly to disrupt the self-sabotage of maladaptive schemas that resonate with old memories of shaming, guilt and limiting beliefs Once freed from negative emotions, clients can use EFT to help them release their emotional blocks and flourish, (Fredrickson & Losada, 2005) enjoying improved wellbeing, relationships, professional success, and financial security.

Stafford had multiple personal experiences using EFT to manage the psychological effects of her whistleblower traumas. She was introduced to EFT by her doctoral coach (co-author, Meier) in 2011 just after she began dealing with the stress of reporting the corruption in her organization to the district attorney. Although her psychotherapist was treating her with n-CBT and she was taking antidepressants, she was still overwhelmed, deeply depressed, and obsessed with what would happen to her after she lost her job. Meier taught her a version of EFT that she could use covertly in meetings, tapping on hand accupoints, enabling her to stay centered and focused on what she needed to do. Stafford describes how using EFT empowered her be resilient in stressful situations.

Use of Emotional Freedom Techniques (EFT)

Stafford: When I was meeting with the District Attorney, using tapping along with the mindfulness and affirmation statements, I was able to create a mental, "cool down space." My heart rate slowed down, my breathing deepened, and my shoulders relaxed. It felt like a great load had been lifted.

Stafford: I use tapping regularly now as a stress resilience practice. Tapping is empowering. It gives me something I can do anytime I start feeling overwhelmed. It disrupts my downward emotional spiral, giving me a respite in a place where there is no rest. With regular practice, it works faster. I don't have to do as many rounds.

Conclusion

In this chapter, we have illustrated how even high functioning professionals, who courageously took the ethical stance and confronted organizational corruption by blowing the whistle, could be deeply traumatized by their employers' Machiavellian retaliation tactics. We have gone deep into the neuropsychology of psychological traumatization to describe how it is expressed across whistleblowers' biological, psychological, and social systems. This type of analysis illustrates the multilevel damage and gives voice to survivors about the suffering such traumas inflicted, as well as the coping strategies they used in order to recover. It also demonstrates the value of understanding these complex neurological systems as the empirical basis for different kinds of trauma-informed psychotherapeutic strategies. Since the need for whistleblowers is increasing, the good news for such future whistleblowers is that that there are now effective ways to restore hope and support their efforts to be resilient.

References

American Headache Society. (2016, May 18). Post-Traumatic Stress Disorder (PTSD) & migraine. Retrieved November 4, 2017, from https://americanheadachesociety.org/news/post-traumatic-stress-disorder-ptsd-migraine/

Anxiety and Depression Association of America. (n.d.). Posttraumatic Stress Disorder (PTSD). Retrieved February 26, 2018, from https://adaa.org/understanding-anxiety/posttraumatic-stress-disorder-ptsd

Atkinson, R. C., & Shiffrin, R. M. (1968). Human memory: A proposed system and its control processes. In K. W. Spence & J. T. Spence (Eds.), *Psychology of Learning and Motivation: Advances in Research and Theory* (Vol. 2, pp. 89–195). Elsevier. https://doi.org/10.1016/S0079- 7421(08)60422-3

Baddeley, A. (1986). *Working Memory*. New York: Oxford University Press.

Barsaglini, A., Sartori, G., Benetti, S., Pettersson-Yeo, W., & Mechelli, A. (2013). The effects of psychotherapy on brain function: A systematic and critical review. *Progress in Neurobiology, 114*. https://doi.org/10.1016/j.pneurobio.2013.10.006

Bauer, P. J. (2013). Memory development. In J. L. R. Rubenstein & P. Rakic (Eds.), *Neural Circuit Development and Function in the Brain* (pp. 297–314). Elsevier. https://doi.org/10.1016/B978-0-12-397267-5.09994-5

Beck, J., Freeman, A., Pretzer, J., Davis, D. D., Flemming, B., Ottavani, R., ... Trexler, L. (1990). *Cognitive Therapy of Personality Disorders. New York City: Guilford Press.*

Beck, & Haigh, E. A. P. (2014). Advances in cognitive theory and therapy: The Generic Cognitive Model. *Annual Review of Clinical*

Psychology, 10(1), 1–24. https://doi.org/10.1146/annurev-clin-psy-032813-153734

Beck Institute for Cognitive Behavior Therapy. (n.d.). *Cognitive Model.* Retrieved December 31, 2017, from https://beckinstitute. org/cognitive-model/

Becker, C., & Zayfert, C. (2001). Integrating DBT-based techniques and concepts to facilitate exposure treatment for PTSD. *Cognitive and Behavioral Practice*, 8(2), pp. 107–122. https://doi. org/10.1016/S1077-7229(01)80017-1

Behbehani, M. (1995). Functional characteristics of the midbrain periaqueductal gray. *Progress in Neurobiology*, 46(6), pp. 575–605.

Bjorkelo, B. (2013). Workplace bullying after whistleblowing: future research and implications. *Journal of Managerial Psychology*, 28, pp. 306–323.

Bjørkelo, B., Einarsen, S., & Matthiesen, S. (2010). Predicting proactive behaviour at work: Exploring the role of personality as an antecedent of whistleblowing behaviour. *Journal of Occupational and Organizational Psychology*, 83(2), pp. 371–394. https://doi.org/10.1348/096317910X486385

Bjørkelo, B., Ryberg, W., & Einarsen, S. (2008). 'When you talk and talk and nobody listens': A mixed method case studies of whistleblowing and its consequences. *International Journal of Organisational Behavior*, 13(2), pp. 18–40. Retrieved from https://www.researchgate.net/profile/Stale_Einarsen/publication/260600129_When_you_talk_and_talk_and_nobody_listens_A_mixed_method_case_study_of_whistleblowing_and_its_consequences/links/5627842008aea4ef176debee.pdf

Blascovich, J., & Tomaka, J., (1996). The Biopsychosocial model of arousal regulation. *Advances in Experimental Social Psychology, 28,* 1-52. https://doi.org/10.1016/S0065-2601(08)60235-X

Blascovich, J., Mendes, W., Tomaka, J., Salomon, K., & Seery, M.

(2003). The robust nature of the biopsychosocial model challenge and Threat: A reply to Wright and Kirby. *Personality and Social Psychology Review*, 7(3), pp. 234–243. https://doi.org/10.1207/S15327957PSPR0703_03

Bonanno, G. (2004). Loss, trauma, and human resilience: Have we underestimated the human capacity to thrive after extremely aversive events? *American Psychologist*, 59, pp. 20–28.

Bouret, S., & Sara, S. (2010). Locus coeruleus. *Scholarpedia*, 5(3), 2845. https://doi.org/10.4249/scholarpedia.2845

Brewin, C., Gregory, J., Lipton, M., & Burgess, N. (2010). Intrusive images in psychological disorders: Characteristics, neural mechanisms, and treatment implications. *Psychological Review*, 117(1), pp. 210–232. https://doi.org/10.1037/a0018113

Calhoun, L.G., Cann, A., & Tedeschi, R.G. (2010). The posttraumatic growth model: Socio-cultural considerations. In T. Weiss & R. Berger, (Eds.), *Posttraumatic growth and culturally competent practice: Lessons learned from around the globe.* (pp. 1-14). Hoboken, NJ: Wiley. ISBN: 978-0-470-35802-3

Campbell, J. (2008). *The hero with a thousand faces*. Princeton: Princeton University Press, 1968, p. 30 / Novato, California: New World Library, 2008. Princeton, NJ: New World Library.

Center for Substance Abuse Treatment. (2014). *Trauma Informed Care in Behavioral Health Services* (Treatment Improvement Protocol Series No. No.57). Rockville, MD: Substance Abuse and Mental Health Services Administration.

Chedekel, L. (2012, May 21). *'Magic' antidepressant may hold promise for PTSD*. Retrieved August 3, 2018, from http://c-hit.org/2012/05/31/magic_antidepressant_may_hold_promise_for_ptsd/

Church, D. (2014, October). *Peak Performance Online Symposium*. Presented at the Peak Performance Online Summit, Dawson Church, Host.

Church, D., & Feinstein, D. (2013). Energy psychology in the treatment of PTSD: Psychobiology and clinical principles. In T. van Leeuwen & M. Brouwer (Eds.), *The Psychology of Trauma*, pp. 211–224. Hauppauge, New York: Nova Science Publishers. Retrieved from https://www.researchgate.net/profile/Dawson_Church2/publication/287303921_Energy_psychology_in_the_treatment_of_PTSD_Psychobiology_and_clinical_principles/links/57bb278f08ae51eef1f3cdbb.pdf

Cortois, C., & Ford, J. (2009). Overview: History of trauma theory. In *Trauma: Contemporary Directions in Theory, Practice and Research.* pp. 1–12. Sage Publications. Retrieved from https://www.sagepub.com/sites/default/files/upm-binaries/40688_1.pdf

Craig, S. (2014, October 24). *The effects of trauma on working memory.* Retrieved April 13, 2018, from https://meltdownstomastery.wordpress.com/2014/10/24/the-effects-of-trauma-on-working-memory/

Davidson, K., & Sherod, K. (2013). Aspects. In D. Church & S. Marohn (Eds.), *Clinical EFT Handbook* (Kindle e-book) (2nd ed., Vol. 1). Energy Psychology Press.

Department of Veterans Affairs. (2017). VA/DOD *Clinical Practice Guideline for the Management of Posttraumatic Stress Disorder and Acute Stress Disorder*. Department of Defense. Retrieved from https://www.healthquality.va.gov/guidelines/MH/ptsd/VADoDPTSDCPGFinal012418.pdf

Dudai, Y. (2004). The neurobiology of consolidations: Or, how stable is the engram? *Annual Review of Psychology*, 55(1), pp. 51–86. https://doi.org/10.1146/annurev.psych.55.090902.142050

Ecker, B. (2011, January 13*). Reconsolidation: A Universal, Integrative Framework for Highly Effective Psychotherapy - Psychotherapy Treatment And Psychotherapist Information*. Retrieved February 16, 2018, from https://www.mentalhelp.net/blogs/

reconsolidation-a-universal-integrative-framework-for-high-ly-effective-psychotherapy/

Ecker, B., Ticic, R., & Hulley, L. (2012). *Unlocking the emotional Brain: Eliminating symptoms at their roots using memory reconsolidation.* New York; London: Routledge.

Ecker, B., Ticic, R., & Hulley, L. (2013). A primer on memory reconsolidating and its psychotherapeutic use as a core process of profound change. *The Neuropsychotherapist*, 1. https://doi.org/10.12744/tnpt(1)082-099

Feinstein, D. (2010). Rapid treatment of PTSD: Why psychological exposure with acupoint tapping may be effective. *Psychotherapy: Theory, Research, Practice, Training*, 47(3), pp. 385–402. https://doi.org/10.1037/a0021171

Field, T., Beeson, E., & Jones, L. (2015). The new ABCs: A practitioner's guide to neuroscience-Informed Cognitive-Behavior Therapy. *Journal of Mental Health Counseling*, 37(3), pp. 206–220. https://doi.org/10.17744/1040-2861-37.3.206

Fredrickson, B., & Losada, M. (2005). Positive affect and the complex dynamics of human flourishing. *American Psychologist*, 60(7), pp. 678–686. https://doi.org/10.1037/0003-066X.60.7.678

Galea, S., Nandi, A., & Vlahov, D. (2005). The epidemiology of post-traumatic stress disorder after disasters. *Epidemiologic Reviews*, 27(1), pp. 78–91. https://doi.org/10.1093/epirev/mxi003

Gilboa, A., & Marlatte, H. (2017). Neurobiology of schemas and schema-mediated memory. *Trends in Cognitive Sciences,* 21(8), pp. 618–631. https://doi.org/10.1016/j.tics.2017.04.013

Glaser, R., & Kiecolt-Glaser, J. (2005). Stress-induced immune dysfunction: Implications for health. *Nature Reviews Immunology*, 5(3), pp. 243–251. https://doi.org/10.1038/nri1571

Hamid, M., & Othman, Z. (2015). Whistleblowing and voicing dissent in organizations. *International Journal of Management Sci-*

ences, 6(1), pp. 8–15.

Hayes, S., Luoma, J., Bond, F., Masuda, A., & Lillis, J. (2006). Acceptance and Commitment Therapy: Model, processes and outcomes. *Behaviour Research and Therapy*, 44(1), pp. 1–25. https://doi.org/10.1016/j.brat.2005.06.006

Hollowood, T. (2018, January 24). *Short term memory*. Retrieved April 13, 2018, from https://simplypsychology.org/short-term-memory.html

Janoff-Bulman, R. (2002). *Shattered Assumptions: Towards a New Psychology of Trauma*. New York: The Free Press.

Jeffreys, M. (2017). *Clinician's guide to medications for PTSD*. Retrieved December 12, 2017, from https://www.ptsd.va.gov/professional/treatment/overview/clinicians-guide-to-medications-for-ptsd.asp#symptoms

Kaiser, E., Gillette, C., & Spinazzola, J. (2010). A controlled pilot-outcome study of sensory integration (SI) in the treatment of complex adaptation to traumatic stress. *Journal of Aggression, Maltreatment & Trauma*, 19(7), pp. 699–720. https://doi.org/1 0.1080/10926771.2010.515162

Kandel, E., & Schwartz, J. H. (1982). Molecular biology of learning: Modulation of transmitter release. *Science*, 218(29), pp. 413–442. Retrieved from http://www.neurosci.info/courses/systems/LearningCellular/Kandel_82_Molecular.pdf

Karatzias, T., Jowett, S., Begley, A., & Deas, S. (2016). Early maladaptive schemas in adult survivors of interpersonal trauma: foundations for a cognitive theory of psychopathology. *European Journal of Psychotraumatology*, 7(1), pp. 30713. https://doi.org/10.3402/ejpt.v7.30713

Karl, A., Schaefer, M., Malta, L., Dörfel, D., Rohleder, N., & Werner, A. (2006). A meta-analysis of structural brain abnormalities in PTSD. *Neuroscience and Biobehavioral Reviews*, 30(7), pp. 1004–1031. https://doi.org/10.1016/j.neubiorev.2006.03.004

Kessler, R. (1995). Posttraumatic stress disorder in the National Co-morbidity Survey. *Archives of General Psychiatry*, 52(12), 1048. Retrieved from https://www.researchgate.net/profile/ Michael_Hughes50/publication/15707358_Posttraumat-ic_Stress_Disorder_in_the_National_Comorbidity_Survey/ links/5a6878c40f7e9b7a554bf717/Posttraumatic-Stress-Dis-order-in-the-National-Comorbidity-Survey.pdf

Kira, I., Ashby, J., Omidy, A., & Lewandowski, L. (2015). Current, continuous, and cumulative trauma-focused cognitive behav-ior therapy: A new model for trauma counseling. *Journal of Mental Health Counseling*, 37(4), pp. 323–340. https://doi. org/10.17744/mehc.37.4.04

Klarik, M., Kvesic, A., Mandic, V., Petrov, B., & Franciskovic, T. (2013). Secondary traumatization and systemic traumatic stress. *Medicina Academica Mostariensia*, 1(1), pp. 29–36. Retrieved from http://www.hdbp.org/psychiatria_danubina/ pdf/dnb_vol25_sup1/dnb_vol25_sup1_29.pdf

Kline, R. (2014, March 18). Whistleblowers who raise concerns still at risk of losing their jobs. *The Guardian*. Retrieved from https:// www.theguardian.com/healthcare-network/2014/mar/18/ whistleblowers-raise-concerns-jobs-loss-nhs

Lawson, G. (2005). The Hero's journey as a developmental meta-phor in counseling. *The Journal of Humanistic Counseling*, Education and Development, 44(2), pp. 134–144. https://doi. org/10.1002/j.2164-490X.2005.tb00026.x

LeDoux, J. (2015, August 10). *The amygdala is NOT the brain's fear center*. Retrieved May 30, 2018, from https://www.psycholo-gytoday.com/blog/i-got-mind-tell-you/201508/the-amygdala-is-not-the-brains-fear-center

Levine, P. (2012). *In an unspoken voice*. Berkeley, California: North Atlantic Books. Retrieved from https://books.google. com/books?hl=en&lr=&id=ie09As4SaLMC&oi=fnd&p-

g=PR11&dq=In+an+unspoken+voice:+How+the+body+re-
leases+trauma+and+restores+goodness.+&ots=7ix1OI08Y-
H&sig=3CyDezTYtkpWAUfdzwGSOjSKOs8#v=onep-
age&q=In%20an%20unspoken%20voice%3A%20How%20
the%20body%20releases%20trauma%20and%20restores%20
goodness.&f=false

Maier, S., & Seligman, M. (2016). Learned helplessness at fifty: Insights from neuroscience. *Psychological Review*, 123(4), pp.
349–367. https://doi.org/10.1037/rev0000033

Malin, L. (2018). *Types of memory: Declarative memory (explicit memory) and procedural memory (implicit memory)*. Retrieved April 21, 2018, from http://www.human-memory.net/
types_declarative.html

Manitoba Trauma Information and Education Centre. (n.d.). *Trauma
and its effects: Fight/flight/freeze*. Retrieved May 16, 2018,
from https://trauma-informed.ca/trauma-and-its-effects-fight-
flight-freeze/

Mann, M. (2018). Learning and memory. *The Nervous System in Action*. Retrieved April 7, 2018, from http://michaeldmann.net/
mann18.html

Maslin, L. (2018a). *Memory processes: Memory consolidation*. Retrieved April 23, 2018, from http://www.human-memory.net/
processes_consolidation.html

Maslin, l. (2018b). *Memory processes: Memory recall/retrieval*. Retrieved May 3, 2018, from http://www.human-memory.net/
processes_recall.html

Maslin, L. (2018c). *Types of memory: Episodic memory and semantic memory*. Retrieved April 18, 2018, from http://www.hu-
man-memory.net/types_episodic.html

Maxfield, L., & Solomon, R. (2017, July 31). *Eye movement desensitization and reprocessing (EMDR) therapy*. Retrieved March
2, 2018, from http://www.apa.org/ptsd-guideline/treatments/

eye-movement-reprocessing.aspx

McLeod, S. (2007). *Stages of memory encoding, storage and retrieval.* Retrieved April 13, 2018, from https://simplypsychology.org/memory.html

Mesmer-Magnus, J., & Viswesvaran, C. (2005). Whistleblowing in organizations: An examination of correlates of whistleblowing intentions, actions, and retaliation. *Journal of Business Ethics,* 62(3), pp. 277–297. https://doi.org/10.1007/s10551-005-0849-1

Mont, J. (2012, September 18). *The whistleblower retaliation epidemic.* Retrieved August 28, 2018, from https://www.complianceweek.com/news/news-article/the-whistleblower-retaliation-epidemic#.W4XCa5NKigz

National Institute of Mental Health. (2016, February). *Post-traumatic stress disorder.* Retrieved August 3, 2018, from https://www.nimh.nih.gov/health/topics/post-traumatic-stress-disorder-ptsd/index.shtml

Overcash, W. S., Calhoun, L. G., Cann, A., & Tedeschi, R. G. (1996). Coping with crises: An examination of the impact of traumatic events on religious beliefs. *Journal of Genetic Psychology,* 157(4), 455-464 journals.sagepub.com/doi/abs/10.1177/153476560401000403

Ozer, E., Best, S., Lipsey, T., & Weiss, D. (2003). Predictors of post-traumatic stress disorder and symptoms in adults: A meta-analysis. *Psychological Bulletin,* 129(1), pp. 52–73. https://doi.org/10.1037/0033-2909.129.1.52

Pearlman, L., & Saakvitne, K. (1995). *Trauma and the therapist: Countertransference and vicarious traumatization in psychotherapy with incest survivors* (1st ed). New York: Norton.

Porges, S. W. (2001). The polyvagal theory: Phylogenetic substrates of a social nervous system. *International Journal of Psychophysiology,* 42(2), pp. 123–146. https://doi.org/10.1016/S0167-

8760(01)00162-3

Roozendaal, B., McEwen, & Chattarji, S. (2009). Stress, memory and the amygdala. *Nature Reviews Neuroscience*, 10(6), pp. 423–433. https://doi.org/10.1038/nrn2651

Scaer, R. C. (2001). The neurophysiology of dissociation and chronic disease. *Applied Psychophysiology and Biofeedback*, 26(1), pp. 73–91.

Shalev, A., Liberzon, I., & Marmar, C. (2017). Post-traumatic stress disorder. *New England Journal of Medicine*, 376(25), pp. 2459–2469. https://doi.org/10.1056/NEJMra1612499

Shapiro, F. (Ed.). (2002). *EMDR as an integrative psychotherapy approach: Experts of diverse orientations explore the paradigm prism*. Washington, DC: American Psychological Association.

Shin, L., & Liberzon, I. (2010). The neurocircuitry of fear, stress and anxiety disorders. *Neuropsychopharmacology*, 35(1), pp. 169–191. https://doi.org/10.1038/npp.2009.83

Shin, L. M., Shin, P., Heckers, S., Krangel, T., Macklin, M., Orr, S., … Rauch, S. (2004). Hippocampal function in posttraumatic stress disorder. *Hippocampus*, 14(3), pp. 292–300. https://doi.org/10.1002/hipo.10183

Siegel, D. J. (2010). *The mindful therapist: A clinician's guide to mindsight and neural integration*. New York: W.W. Norton & Co.

Siegel, D. J. (2012). *Pocket guide to interpersonal neurobiology: An integrative handbook of the mind*. New York: W.W. Norton & Co.

Simeon, D., Knutelska, M., Yehuda, R., Putnam, F., Schmeidler, J., & Smith, L. M. (2007). Hypothalamic-pituitary-adrenal axis function in dissociative disorders: Post-traumatic stress sisorder, and healthy volunteers. *Biological Psychiatry*, 61(8), pp, 966–973. https://doi.org/10.1016/j.biopsych.2006.07.030

Simiola, V., Neilson, E., Thompson, R., & Cook, J. (2015). Preferences for trauma treatment: A systematic review of the empirical literature. *Psychological Trauma: Theory, Research, Practice, and Policy*, 7(6), pp. 516–524. https://doi.org/10.1037/tra0000038

Smith, A. (n.d.). The elusive rewards and high costs of being a whistleblower. Retrieved September 3, 2018, from http://www.kiplinger.com/article/business/T012-C000-S002-high-costs-of-being-a-whistleblower.html

Sonnier, B., & Lasser, W. (2013). An empirical evaluation of Graham's Model of Principled Organizational Dissent in the whistleblower context Post-SOX. *Journal of Forensic & Investigative Accounting*, 5(2). Retrieved from http://web.nacva.com/JFIA/Issues/JFIA-2013-2_6.pdf

Stafford, R. (2015). A case study of public leaders who whistleblew: Biopsychosocial trajectory for trauma and transformation. In G. D. Sardana & T. Thatchenkery (Eds.), *Optimizing Business Growth: Strategies for Scaling Up.* pp. 471–485. Bloomsbury Publishing.

Stafford, R. (2016a), August). *The shadow side of qualitative research: A researcher's experiences with secondary psychological trauma and posttraumatic growth.* Conference Presentation presented at The European Sociological Association's (ESA) Qualitative Research Methods & Technologies Conference, Jagiellonian University, Krakow, Poland.

Stafford, R. (2016b,) December). *The shadow side of qualitative research: Secondary traumatization as a risk factor.* Conference Presentation presented at the ICMC 2015 Conference, Birla Institute of Management Technology Greater Nodia, India.

Stafford, R. L. (2017). *When public leaders whistleblow: Biopsychosocial trajectory for trauma.* Santa Barbara, CA: Dissertations & Theses @ Fielding Graduate University; ProQuest Dissertations & Theses Global. (1868429801). Retrieved from https://

fgul.idm.oclc.org/login?url=http://search.proquest.com.fgul.
idm.oclc.org/docview/1868429801?accountid=10868

Stafford, R. & Meier, A. (2017). The shadow side of qualitative research: Secondary psychological traumatization as a risk factor. In G. D. Sardana & T. Thatchenkery (Eds.), *Knowledge Creation and Organizational Well-Being: Leveraging Talent Management and Appreciative Intelligence.* pp. 270–281. New Delhi, India: Bloomsbury Publishing.

Stein, D., McLaughlin, K., Koenen, K., Atwoli, L., Friedman, M., Hill, E., … Kessler, R. (2014). DSM-5 and ICD-11 Definitions of posttraumatic stress disorder: investigating "narrow" and "broad" approaches. *Depression and Anxiety*, 31(6), pp. 494–505. https://doi.org/10.1002/da.22279

Tedeschi, R., & Calhoun, L. (2004). Posttraumatic growth: Conceptual foundations and empirical evidence. *Psychological Inquiry*, 15(1), pp. 1–18. https://doi.org/10.1207/s15327965pli1501_01

Tonegawa, S., Liu, X., Ramirez, S., & Redondo, R. (2015). Memory engram cells have come of age. *Neuron*, 87(5), pp. 918–931. https://doi.org/10.1016/j.neuron.2015.08.002

Transparency International. (2017). *What is corruption?* Retrieved August 19, 2018, from https://www.transparency.org/what-is-corruption

Transparency International. (2017). *Corruption in the USA: The difference a year makes.* Retrieved August 19, 2018, from https://www.transparency.org/news/feature/corruption_in_the_usa_the_difference_a_year_makes

Tse, D., Langston, R., Kakeyama, M., Bethus, I., Spooner, P., Wood, E., … Morris, R. (2007). Schemas and memory consolidation. *Science*, 316(5821), pp. 76–82. https://doi.org/10.1126/science.1135935

Tuval-Mashiach, R., Freedman, S., Bargai, N., Boker, R., Hadar, H., & Shalev, A. (2004). Coping with trauma: Narrative and cognitive perspectives. *Psychiatry: Interpersonal and Biological Processes*, 67(3), pp. 280–293. https://doi.org/10.1521/psyc.67.3.280.48977

U.S. Equal Employment Opportunity Commission. (n.d.). Fact sheet: Retaliation based on exercise of Workplace rights Is unlawful. Retrieved September 2, 2018, from https://www.eeoc.gov/eeoc/interagency/fs_retaliation.cfm

van der Kolk, B. (1994). EMDR and the lessons from neuroscience research. Retrieved from http://www.emdr.org.il/dls/1.html

van der Kolk, B. (1997, March 2). Posttraumatic Stress Disorder and memory. Retrieved April 13, 2018, from http://www.psychiatrictimes.com/ptsd/posttraumatic-stress-disorder

Vince, G. (2015, May 26). *Hacking the nervous system*. Retrieved February 13, 2018, from https://medium.com/mosaic-science/hacking-the-nervous-system-8d3e84108693

What Is Coherence Therapy? (n.d.). Retrieved November 19, 2017, from https://coherencetherapy.org/discover/what.htm

What Is Exposure Therapy? (n.d.). Retrieved March 26, 2018, from http://www.apa.org/ptsd-guideline/patients-and-families/exposure-therapy.aspx

Yovell, Y., Bannett, Y., & Shalev, A. (2003). Amnesia for traumatic events among recent survivors: A pilot study. *CNS Spectrums*, 8(09), pp. 676–685. https://doi.org/10.1017/S1092852900008865

Appendix

Trauma-Informed Psychotherapies

Association for Comprehensive Energy Psychology https://www.energypsych.org/

Coherence Therapy http://www.coherencetherapy.org/index.htm

EMDR Institute http://www.emdr.com/

National Association of Cognitive Behavioral Therapy (Conventional

CBT) http://www.nacbt.org/

Neuroscience-Informed Cognitive-Behavior Therapy (n-CBT) https://www.n-cbt.com/

Schema Therapy Institute http://www.schematherapy.com/

About the Authors

Rebecca Stafford, PhD is a Developmental Psychologist who has been an advocate for women and children throughout Southern California for four decades. Through her lived professional experiences in health care, government, and non-profit sectors, she has demonstrated her enthusiasm, compassion, and desire to serve, and her passion for public leadership service. Dr. Stafford's dissertation research was inspired by her personal passage as a whistleblower who experienced employer retribution. Her restorative journey led to a keen understanding about whistleblowers who have experienced psychological trauma. She has identified paths to restoration that encompass fearless authenticity and transformative growth.

Building on her process insights, Stafford's practice and research emphasize integrative, interdisciplinary interventions to help whistleblowers learn effective biopsychosocial- centered coping in response to their psychological traumas. The aim of these interventions is to encourage reconciliation, reframing, and reintegration for abiding physical, emotional, and social well-being. Dr. Stafford is internationally known presenter and author. Her work draws awareness to the life altering aftermaths endured by whistleblowers who have experienced retaliation, while emphasizing strategies that support their resilience and recovery. Dr. Stafford may be contacted at rebeccastafford@verizon.net.

Andrea Meier, EdM, PhD is a retired Associate Research Professor from the University of North Carolina (UNC) School of Social Work in

Chapel Hill, NC. While there she specialized in intervention research projects, in particular, technology-mediated (phone and Internet) interventions. She is widely published in the areas of stress resilience and health promotion. Prior to earning her doctorate and., later, joining the UNC faculty, she earned an EdM in Counseling and Consulting Psychology at the Harvard School of Education where she received training in cognitive behavioral therapy. Subsequently, she applied this expertise in her work as a certified substance abuse counselor and trainer for eight years Worcester, MA.

Since retiring from UNC in 2008, Dr. Meier has been in practice (doing business as Flourish! Personal Coaching) offering life coaching services in Boulder, CO. She has earned her International Coach Federation Professional Coach Certification. Among her specialties are: doctoral coaching (including over 50 Fielding Graduate University clients), wellness coaching, and energy psychology coaching (including Emotional Freedom Techniques). As a result of her doctoral coaching work with Rebecca Stafford on her dissertation study, she has consulted and collaborated with Stafford on other whistleblower posttraumatic growth-related articles and international conference presentations. Dr. Meier may be contacted at flourishwithcoaching@gmail.com.

CHAPTER 3

VOICES OF WOMEN: OPPRESSION AND RESILIENCE

Trisha Gentle, EdD
Fielding Graduate University Alumna

Abstract

This chapter describes the demonstrated resilience shared by a diverse pool of women who self-identified as having been oppressed. Women between the ages of 18 and 83 were interviewed for a dissertation research project. Their deeply powerful narratives exposed abuse and oppression across gender, sexual orientation, age, economics, religion/culture, and violence. Contained in the narratives were also a wide range of resilience-building strategies. From learning to respect themselves, to seeking therapeutic support, to becoming an activist, each woman described a personal journey to regaining her life and sense of resilience. Regardless of the approach to healing and resilience, the women each discussed the reality of constantly living with the impact that oppression had in their lives and described a dual existence of working to heal themselves while continuing to deal with its daily presence. These stories of resilience-building in the midst of deeply difficult circumstances offer hope and inspiration.

Keywords: oppression, intersectionality, empowerment, equality, institutional and systemic oppression, inequality, resilience, survival, overcoming, healing

Introduction

Although this dissertation research (Gentle-Wilemon, 2016) began as an exploration of the intersectionality of oppression in women's lives, there were secondary discoveries gathered from the expressive and decidedly open dialogues shared. Specifically, when prompted to discuss gained insights, stories of strength, resolve, and deep resilience were exposed. The types of healing and resilience each woman identified demonstrated a common theme of searching for ways to understand the oppressions experienced and to integrate these experiences into their lives in ways that were on a scale of tolerance, acceptance, and deepened consciousness.

Recent research on resilience identifies adaptive systems in which people live their lives and examines the ability to engage in effective responses to critical events (Greene & Dubus, 2017). Traumatic events such as one-time and continued oppressions can lead to a mixture of negative and positive experience. While experiencing the painful aftermath of oppression is difficult, there is the rise of much internal strength and courage that bring life-long change (Konvisser, 2015).

Within the context of this study, oppression was defined as a profoundly complex and systemic issue deeply embedded within social attitudes, contexts, and structures that create a paradigm of power and control over a person or group of people (Goduka & Geisthardt, 2008).

Oppression intersects across all aspects of an individual's life and its complexity is increased through the multiplicity of experiences (Collins, 2015). This intersectionality became clear throughout the gathering of these women's experiences. Shared experiences of violence, sexism, economic poverty, and racism proved common. The most profound thread of oppression was that of racism. It became clear that racism is deep-seated in our society and continues to have far-reaching consequences.

Methodology

Giving voice to women and bearing witness to their experiences can be one of the most essential elements of transforming the systemic, institutionalized, and continued oppression of women as a group. The research question guiding this study was, "How has oppression impacted the lives of women over the age of 18 who self-identify as having experienced oppression?"

This study was purposefully anchored in feminist theory to give greater priority to hearing and understanding how women interpret and understand their own experiences. Smart (2009) explained the importance of maintaining a core sociological approach to research even in the face of a strong allegiance to textual analysis and theoretical work. She posited the importance of collecting in-depth interview data that bring a richness and complexity to understanding direct experiences. Implementing narrative inquiry through one to two-hour interviews successfully resulted in deep, organic sharing of experiences.

Recruitment

Recruitment efforts included individual dialogues regarding the project, utilizing social media, inviting participants from other group events, snowballing, word of mouth, and some convenience sampling. The final study included 12 women from varied backgrounds, geographical locations, and circumstances. Although we cannot draw definitive conclusions from this relatively small sample, their powerful stories of resilience in the face of difficult and ever-present oppressions are illuminating and provide a foundation of understanding on the intersectionality of various oppressions and their impact.

As way of brief introduction to the participants, please see Table 1. Participant names have been changed.

Data analysis

Research was comprised of interviews with open-ended questions, along

113

with transcriptions of video-tapings, and field notes. Data was analyzed to elicit a cross-representation of perspectives among all participants. There was an exploration of collective content and identification of common threads reaching across each interview. Coding, key words in context, and constant comparison were utilized to develop themes and trends across all data resulting in prevalent similarities in the participant's experiences. This process exposed five predominant intersectional themes for all participants: sexism, economic poverty, violence, racism, and resilience.

Table 1 - Participant Demographics

Participant	Demographic information
Rosa	78-year-old African American woman
Willow	18-year old woman of mixed race and identifies as Black
Barb	83-year-old Jewish woman
Abida	40-year-old Egyptian woman
Tina	38-year-old African American woman
Monique	58-year-old Caucasian woman
Donna	65-year-old African American woman
Dorothy	60-year-old African American woman
Angeline	58-year-old African American woman
Maria	40-year-old Caucasian woman
Teresa	21-year-old Caucasian woman
Imani	45-year-old African American woman

Findings

This section and the next are dedicated to the direct disclosures of participants within each of the five thematic areas. Due to the depth of intersectionality of oppression, it is impossible to separate out how each participant integrated resilience across themes so deeply intertwined and hence this is addressed separately. Their personal discovery and integration of resilience is best demonstrated through the power of their own testimony.

Sexism

The first area of sexism was found to contain ubiquitous, often subtle, yet demeaning experiences felt to be inevitable for a woman in this society. The following three examples are representative of participants' common experiences:

Barb said, "[Sexism] primarily relates to the era I grew up in. It was the model for the fifties." She suffered silently through decades of an abusive marriage – regarded as a norm for some women at the time. Regardless of her own internal doubts, she shared, "My peers were not questioning it, so I stayed quiet as well." Barb shared two primary events that woke up her consciousness and enabled her journey out of the sexist, controlling oppression that had been her life. The first was reading Betty Friedan's The Feminine Mystique.

> This book completely changed my life. I was feeling crazy because I was seeing and feeling things that I was told I shouldn't be. I could not understand why I was so unhappy inside and as I read each page I began to feel… wait a minute… I am not crazy at all! (Barb)

The second trigger was more subtle and profound.

> I had to have a gall bladder surgery and I went to Kaiser, nice but nothing fancy, hospital. And I was treated just like any other patient and I realized this was ten times nicer than I was being treated in my own home. I mean, I could not believe it. They were asking me how I felt, they were respecting my an- swers and it really blew my mind! I knew right then, I had to get out of there (Barb).

Reflecting on the ever-present impact of sexism in women's lives, Willow shared:

> I feel like every woman has at least gotten cat-called at least once walking down the street and not doing anything…the majority of it that I see, and face first hand, has been in school and it has been from stu-

dents but it has been supported by administration and teachers. (Willow)

Teresa had a more intense struggle with the constant sexism she encounters in her job and how her managers are complicit in supporting it by not addressing it. She stated:

I mean it is a corporate hotel and we wear like long-sleeved, buttoned-up shirts and flats...nothing even slightly promiscuous about that outfit, not that it would matter. I have had men say really incredibly rude things to me and I've told them please leave and they'll just sit there and continue to make comments to me. Then, when I talked to my manager about that, my manager's a woman, she told me that's what comes with the job. You just have to accept it. It makes me hate my job even though I really love my job. It's just like you constantly feel unsafe because you get objectified constantly. I live in a constant state of fear of safety and self-hate for being female. (Teresa)

Economic Poverty

Similar to the ingrained experiences of sexism, economic poverty was disproportionately experienced by participants. From the struggles Barb encountered in times prior to women's ability to be financially independent to the deep-seated oppression that created opportunity for exploitation and violence in exchange for simply surviving, their experiences were often severe. Barb provided a historical perspective.

In my era, women were not allowed to have bank accounts, credit cards, or any financial assets in their own name. It was very difficult for women to obtain divorces and to leave with any resources of their own to rebuild their lives. I remember at one point I had a

garage sale to buy food for the week, but we made it
through, all of us (Beth).

As Monique struggled to address her rape-induced post-traumatic stress, she was faced with a cancer diagnosis and chemotherapy. As she began to stabilize, she discovered an unfaithful husband who had lied about maintaining her mortgage and bills during her illness and her home was lost. Monique experienced years of homelessness and struggle before achieving stability.

For Tina, deep poverty was a constant throughout her life. She described how her neighborhood devolved from one of family to drugs and danger. Tina had gotten out of this environment and into an apartment of her own, so her children would not be harmed. However, the conditions remained atrocious and her children dropped to the floor for safety anytime a popping sound occurred. Regardless of her hard work, she remains in poverty today.

Rosa described growing up in poverty that was far beyond that experienced by other participants.

> It was days went by there is no food at all, nothing.
> So, my grandmother used to send me to her sister's
> house just to get a little piece of the cut fat meat
> and she gives me a couple of peas or something like
> that and you know that's how we made it the whole
> winter time. It would just really-really; it was worst
> of the worst. It was the worst thing you can ever think
> up that's hard. (Rosa)

Violence

Violence was a thread that entered every participant's experience and came in many variations, severities, and occurrences. Abida shared her experience with oppression in the form of cultural practices.

> The first oppression I had in my life was when my
> family decided to do female genital mutilation for

117

> me when I was in the age of I think 10. It was not my
> choice you know. They forced me to do that. Even I
> was crying and told them I don't want to do that, you
> know…I was very scared, but they forced me, you
> know. It was extremely painful and, of course, still
> creates physical problems today. (Abida)

Teresa stated: "I was molested by one of my mother's boyfriend when I was nine years old. My older sister was forced to have full intercourse with the same man." While Teresa understood her sister's assault she stated: "I felt like because I 'only' got touched and not penetrated, my trauma did not rise to the level of importance that I felt inside." She described feeling much internal humiliation, self-blame, and confusion.

Monique shared a devastating experience of rape when she was only 18 years of age. Coming from an almost picture-perfect farm upbringing, Monique decided she wanted to serve her country, so she joined the Air Force.

> I had decided to serve my country, so I joined the Air
> Force. So, in 1983 I was in training working towards
> my degree in accounting and finance. On the morning
> of my midterm, I went out for my 4-a.m. run. Only
> on this morning I was suddenly attacked by two men
> who severely beat me, raped me, and left me for
> dead. (Monique)

Monique discussed her continued experiences with the military institutional system.

> There was no acceptance of what happened to me. I
> tried to report it three different times to higher and
> higher officers and was told that I had not been raped
> and that I needed to stop bringing it up. [They] were
> all clear with me that I was going to be discharged if I
> didn't stop pushing it. I lost one of my good conduct

> medals because I tried to get justice… they sent me
> back to class so I had to sit there every day watching
> the guys and trying to figure out which ones had done
> this to me. (Monique)

Maria described living most of her life predominantly free of oppression. Then she experienced a devastating date rape and the subsequent re-victimization of the system that responded to her case. She remains deeply impacted today.

> Yeah, and it's been 5 years now, and I feel like I'm in
> a good spot, but I also wonder like I don't know, will
> there be a time when this is not like fundamentally
> something that I see in myself? Like I really feel like
> I was irrevocably changed. (Maria)

Tina has seen life-long violence and poverty and her response when asked to share her experience with oppression was, "I don't know where to start, that is a lot." Tina then began to reflect on her life beginning at the age of 14 when she was raped by two brothers from her neighborhood. They tricked her into their car under the pretense of taking her to where her cousins were. This rape was violent and included a gun used in terrifying ways. She said, "I was terrified, devastated, and I told no one."

Her second experience with rape began a year later when she was 15. She described the perpetrator as her best friend's father.

> He was the Director of the Community Center and he
> was a well-respected and well-known guy. Everyone
> admired him. They admired the cars he drove, the
> money he made. He was set out as a mentor to the
> youth in the community. But the reality was he raped
> and beat me for years while telling me that if I ever
> told anyone, he'd kill me and pay for my funeral. I
> had seen him do that in more than one occasion with
> others. I got pregnant from the rape and he forced me

> to get an abortion, and I hemorrhaged and bled out so
> badly, I had to be hospitalized. (Tina)

Tina continued sharing.

> On my mom's deathbed she decided to tell me that
> she apologized for selling me to this man. For all
> those years I just thought I was being abused by him,
> that he just found a way to work his way into my life
> and then control me from that point not knowing that
> he paid my mother for all that time. This was a seri-
> ous blow because that came hours before she passed
> away. (Tina)

When Rosa was asked to share her experiences with oppression, she poignantly sat up in her chair, leaned forward, and after a significant pause, related:

> Well, really, I would have to start from the begin-
> ning. My great-grandmother was a very light-skinned
> house slave. After she was freed, she left her teenage
> children and went back to live with the White people.
> So, my grandmother, light-skinned herself, had a
> lot of angriness in her. When they freed slaves, they
> couldn't do nothing for the mind because she still
> have slave mentality, brought it over to her children.
> She didn't like dark children. She made a difference.
> If they were light they can get everything, they can
> sleep in a bed with her and everything, but if they
> were dark she won't want nothing to do with them.
> (Rosa)

Rosa's own mother was dark-skinned and her grandmother sold her out to married men for money, food, and other things. Rosa's mother became pregnant with her as a result of one of these encounters. She remembers as a young child her mother attempting suicide and then one day literally running away toward the train station. Rosa ran after her begging to be taken with her. Her mother refused but told her she would be back. Rosa stated, "She never came back for me." Her mother wound up marrying a man that she did not love just to get out but he "was nothing but a drunk and he beat her all the time."

Rosa was left with her abusive grandmother whom she described as particularly cruel because of Rosa's dark skin tone. Her grandmother had another daughter just a few years younger than Rosa. She was a light-skinned, worshipped child that Rosa experienced as her responsibility to protect and take unending abuse for. Rosa shared story after story of the cruel abuse occurring at the hands of her grandmother. Strikingly, she shared, "I have never experienced love, never heard any kind words but on Sunday, everyone was a Christian and I never got beatings on Sundays. I still say to this day, thank God for every Sunday."

Rosa's life continued to include abuse. She was battered by her husband and found out that he had been sexually molesting her daughter for over ten years. Remembering that time, Rosa quietly stated, "Oh man, that thing almost kill me. It almost kill me. The pain is still there." Rosa's abuse is far from over, as she disclosed that her husband is still abusive today.

Racism

Racism was a pervasive aspect of life for the woman of color in this research. These experiences were profound, ever-present, and deeply damaging to one's sense of being valued and viewed as equal in society. Participants discussed how impossible it is to separate out the issue of racism from other types of oppression such as economic poverty, limited job opportunities, homophobia, and violence. Such an experience of intersectionality was well-articulated by Dorothy.

> I have had people attempt to jump me on the street
> because I am a very butch woman, so it's not like
> people can't tell. I've had folks follow me into public
> restrooms. I've had bottles and rocks thrown at me.

> Were these experiences based on my race, my gender,
> or my sexual identity, or all of the above? I mean,
> education, health, food, housing, all of those systems
> have been a burden to me, so it is kind of hard to de-
> lineate because it's everywhere, it is in everything...
> but for me everything rides on my Blackness. All of
> these other oppressions lean on my Blackness.
> (Dorothy)

Willow shared racist experiences within her own bi-racial family. With frustration, she explained,

> While everyone in society will say they are not a
> racist... my interactions in my family...they say I'm
> not racist, but they say things and they do things that
> are, and they don't realize it. They will slip in subtle
> comments like you are not like the other ones...your
> boyfriend doesn't sag his pants, does he? And other
> things like you are just the sassy Black woman and it
> is not meant as a compliment...I'll be like that's not
> funny...and they don't even understand what they are
> doing is wrong. (Willow)

Imani shared a number of memories of her experiences growing up in Florida and some trips to South Carolina with her mom and sister where they had to sit in the back of the bus. Only two stores would let them come in and shop, but they were allowed in the basement only area of the stores.

> I remember one particular day when we were shop-
> ping, and we were so hot and thirsty. My mom
> attempted to take us in the store just to get a drink
> of water, but this White lady stopped us at the door.
> We tried several stores. Finally, at one store a White
> woman pointed to the door in the back, so my mom
> took us around in the back way. I can still remember

there were Black and White water fountain. I remember my mother took a drink and my sister took a
drink, but I refused. I was too tired and hurt. (Imani)

Angeline, a 58-year-old African American, observed, "I was
born into oppression from the moment I came here. That was being
born Black and female." Indeed, the majority of Angeline's interview
provided one example after another of how racism has permeated her
life. She described a devastating experience of visiting her father's
relatives in the South.

I had one of the worst experiences that I ever had
when I went down south 'cause they had recently...
desegregated the YMCA so we were allowed to go
swimming. Our family was there, and I was sitting on
the side of the pool and these little White boys came
over and urinated on me. My dad was in the
pool with my sister. Now their mothers thought that
was funny and they didn't correct them. I knew better
than to say anything to my father because either my
father was going to kill them, or he was gonna go
to jail and because I did not want to lose my dad. I
stayed silent. That is how oppression works, it silenc-
es your voice even when you know it is wrong and
unfair, but you can't speak and it goes over and over.
(Angeline)

Donna shared significant examples of how racism limited and affected
her life personally.

I've faced oppression at many turns – because I was
Black, because I was female, because I didn't have
secondary education. I was only able to go so far in
the government arena so I moved to private industry.
It may have been even worse there... White women

hired and promoted who had much less experience...
having to sit outside attorneys' offices and listen to
them speak to clients on speakerphones where they
openly and loudly referred to Blacks as niggers ...
subjection to passes and inappropriate behavior from
White male bosses... they knew I needed that job
as a single parent, so they never worried about me
quitting or raising any hell. I was used and pulled out
for Black clients for events that required diversity and
then relegated back to the lower end of the law firm
paid positions once that was over. It was a hard road.
(Donna)

Along with her strong connections with slavery, Rosa also recounted
some specific experiences of racism both growing up and as an adult.

When I was looking for a job in North Virginia, they
had a sign on the door of this store... saying waitress
wanted $25.00 a week. That was back in the '60s...
wow that would be good money for me and my baby.
When I went in there to apply for the job, they tell
me straight up, we want a White girl. Turned down
'cause of my race. They didn't care about hurting my
feelings or nothing like that and I walked out crying.
I said to myself, how come they didn't just put that
in the window? I wouldn't have gone in there. I just
didn't expect that when I moved to Virginia. (Rosa)

Rosa continued:

Down in the country, Black people know their part.
Back in them days we was told if you want to survive
you got to keep yourself humble. They might speak
to you in the field but they ain't gonna do it around
other White folk. One time this White man spit down
on us from the top of a Ferris-wheel ride... but you

can't do nothing... they will kill you. I mean Black
people down there know they place...you know I
still feel it even today you know. Not as bad and I try
to not let stuff like than enter my mind but I feel it.
(Rosa)

Abida spoke about the increased tension and racism she has experienced being a Muslim in America during her current stay here. She sadly described the differences in experiences.

The level of fear, rejection and unkind name-calling
and other intimidating behaviors is greatly exaggerat-
ed from my last visit of only 5 years ago. People have
yelled at me "go home" and "you don't belong here."
This time I really feel it a lot, you know because
many, many things have happened this time. Yes,
this time I feel, many, many things that hurt me. I am
trying to learn how to have thicker skin. I must go on.
(Abida)

The existence of racism and bias was also articulated by a white ally. Maria shared that after a 5-hour grueling interrogation with the police officer she was exhausted and overwhelmed. She thought:

No way was it appropriate that I was treated this way.
What if English was not my first language...what if
I was a sex worker or you know, transgendered....
You know, I mean I carried a whole lot of privilege
with me...I am White, articulate, have experience in
victim services, had not been drinking...I was like oh
my God, if I am getting treated like this... It's like oh
my God, you know? (Maria)

As indicated by each of these participants' life examples, racism is an ever-present experience for those of color. Regardless of the situation, lifestyle, or their incredible contributions to society, they are confronted with the biases of others which intentionally or unintentionally limit opportunities, equality, and can affect their own sense of self-worth.

Resilience

In the face of these profound experiences of oppression, there was a consistent surfacing of coping, understanding, adaptation, and even healing that demonstrates resilience. Each woman described times of devastation, anger, and struggles with coping. Although each journey was individual and had its own progression, a sense of strength and resilience surfaced for each woman. Participants articulated several stages of resilience associated with the different types of trauma they experienced as well as the time period within their healing journey. Often, right after the onset of the trauma, a more reactive, survival-focused resilience and coping were shared.

Barb described her initial steps into resilience: "In the beginning, I just used my mama bear strength, I needed to be strong to save my kids." Barb's description was of learning to value and trust herself. She stated:

> I have tried to speak out and to pass it on to my kids.
> To me it is wonderful to see that my daughter and
> daughter in-laws are all strong women. Stand up for
> yourself. Trust yourself. Find out who you are not
> matter how old you are – that's probably the main
> thing because with oppression you learn to hide that.
> (Barb)

This was representative of others. Maria's remembrance of the immediate aftermath also captured a common experience of initial coping.

> My experience was so much about just surviving,
> getting through the next hour, then the day, then the
> week, at the worst of this. I don't know that I had any
> conscious thoughts about it at the time, other than

to think "Well, it can't get any worse than this . . ."
(Maria)

As distance from the initial trauma increased, others shared experiences of a more long-term integration, and a sense of resilience was seen in life changes and deeper understandings of themselves. Here are their own words.

Imani shared that her life experiences were likely what had brought her to her current work with homeless individuals experiencing mental health concerns. She stated:

> I have survived to this point. I had to be willing to look at the self and that's very, very difficult for most, for many that I have known. You'd be amazed to know how powerful that is so you have to start with the self- finding the healing and peace within. (Imani)

Tina's experiences were similar.

> Over the years, I've learned a lot working in victim services, just educating myself on various levels has helped me to grow and to forgive and to understand. It doesn't change the hurt and pain but it has helped me to move on in life. If I had not gone to victim services.... I would be angry 'cause I would have a whole lot of hurt that I wouldn't understand. (Tina)

Maria described her experiences after the initial trauma this way:

> Looking back at it with more perspective... I think that solidarity with other survivors was really huge for me. I had gotten into a group counseling program through a rape crisis center and knowing that there were another 8 or so survivors I saw on a weekly basis that were going through the same thing was really powerful. And after about three months I had the opportunity to attend a survivor-only sweat lodge experience with about 40 or 50 survivors that were

127

> all much further along in the process and seemed to
> have rebuilt their lives so that was very encouraging.
> I do remember feeling like such a mess and several
> women telling me that was totally normal but that it
> does get better. And it did. I got professional therapy
> too, but I don't think it came close to helping the way
> that just being able to see and talk with others that
> have walked this walk did. (Maria)

Maria moved through each stage of healing by engaging a variety of coping skills. She has moved to a stage of integration that includes successful advocacy efforts bringing legislative change to better support rape victims. Her journey held numerous insights.

> Also, I think my faith helped me through this, but not
> in the sense that one would probably think. I think my
> being raped broke God's heart, and that made me feel
> deeply supported even as I felt deeply lost. I was able
> to connect with a base common humanity that made
> me look differently at the people all around me... I
> felt like I finally stripped away all my ego of my job
> or career or privileged upbringing and just focused
> on being human, no more no less. And I comforted
> myself with knowing that any suffering I experienced
> was something that God/Jesus understood perfectly,
> which made me feel less alone. (Maria)

Maria continued:

> Finally, I have to say that a tremendous amount of
> anger and rage got me through it. I won't pretend
> that I think that was necessarily healthy, but I was
> determined not to let this destroy me any more than it
> already had. (Maria)

There was a third type of resilience that seemed to be present in the stories of the women of color whose experiences of oppression were complicated by the overlay of continual racism. Participants described their struggles to maintain some sense of safety and holding on to their sense of integrity and value as they faced the continuous micro-aggressions of sexism and racism.

In closing, it is important to note that while limited in scope, the sharing from the women in this research underscores a profound ability to heal from unspeakable oppressions. Their willingness to share such open and raw truths about their journeys lends remarkable support to the concept of healing and resilience. The stories seem to create a common language for becoming a survivor and thriver after a devastating event. Here are some of their final words.

> **Tina:** I have been able to navigate my way through life with these things… scars… and these wounds on me. Certain things could trigger me…and I can shut it down. I question is there something wrong with me… but I always get this renewed strength that allows me to push and I get this confidence from somewhere and I become a fighter again and a survivor again and I wore an S on my chest… I can feel like that. A lot to offer.
>
> **Rosa**: They give me a plaque just about a week ago at a block party…. They said I did so much over the years. You encouraged me over the years. So, it is not about talking all the time…it's in the doing. I wrote some goals on the refrigerator so I can look at them; that's really important…this is what I am going for… and keep your strength. You have such strength and courage. Give back.
>
> **Maria:** I feel like I was irrevocably changed… I do feel very proud of what I've accomplished and that if today someone is assaulted… they can go to a sane

exam without having to report it and… if they do report… maybe be treated with compassion… So, maybe a lot of good came out of it…yeah, that's true, there's some good that came out of it.

Donna: Oppressed women need empathy, understanding, compassion from society as a whole, but most importantly from other women. They need patience and time to understand their situation and to seek ways to move through it. They need to be heard, listened to, and commiserated with. They need to be recognized as people going through, but not in a permanent state; people that can grow from their current situation but are not defined by it. We must seek to use our oppression to make a way out, to manipulate, and maneuver it until it is no longer oppression but something that serves and sustains us. To never give up trying to break the shackles of oppression and to continue believing in ourselves. Cry. Forgive. Learn. Move on. Let your tears water the seeds of your future happiness.

Conclusion

Though this dissertation research (Gentle-Wilemon, 2016) focused on the experiences and impact of oppression across multiple aspects of life, there was an unanticipated discovery of commonalities in recovery and resilience for each participant. Journeys to healing were varied in timelines and avenues taken yet each participant independently offered stories of resilience. This resilience manifested at different stages of the healing process and seemed to deepen with time.

Moving forward in accessing the connection between oppression and resilience, it would be meaningful to examine systemic, perpetual oppressions such as racism. The ever-present nature of racism brings a different dimension to the process of healing. When considering resilience within the context of racism, it is essential to acknowledge its ever-present nature. As explained by DeGruy (2005), the work of healing past oppressions must be done while constantly experiencing new oppressions both as individuals and communities of color. Specific to racism, Brown (2008) suggests that ensuring racial pride, a strong sense of self value, and the collective support of extended family and community are all critical components for building resilience.

While it is clear that further exploration of how resilience is reached would be meaningful, an expansion of learning from those who have been oppressed would be of significant value. In addition to considering the skills, types, and progressions of resilience, it would be beneficial to more deeply analyze how finding resilience after a one-time event, multiple events in the past, and the continued oppressions one faces each day differ. Continued work will be richly enhanced by incorporating the individual voices of those who have experienced oppression directly. Honoring the experiences of those who have been oppressed through acknowledging their own stories will expansively provide a deeper understanding of what resilience is.

References

Brown, D.L. (2008). African American resiliency: Examining racial socialization and social support as protective factors. *Journal of Black Psychology, 34*(1), 32-48. doi:10.1177/0095798407310538

Collins, P.H. (2009). *Black feminist thought: Knowledge, consciousness, and the politics of empowerment.* New York, NY: Routledge.

DeGruy, J. (2005). *Post traumatic slave syndrome: America's legacy of enduring injury and healing.* Milwaukie, OR: Uptone Press.

Gentle-Wilemon, P. (2016). *Voices of women: Facing intersectional experiences of oppression* (Doctoral dissertation). Retrieved from ProQuest Dissertations & Theses Global. (Order No. 10255379)

Goduka, I. & Geisthardt, C. (2008). *Social construction of systems of oppression and privilege.* Boston, MA: Pearson Custom.

Greene, R., & Dubus, N. (2017). *Resilience in action: An information and practice guide.* Washington, DC: NASW Press.

Konvisser, Z.D. (2015). "What happened to me can happen to anybody" – Women exonerees speak out. *Texas A&M Law Review,* 3, 303-366.

Smart, C. (2009). Shifting horizons: Reflections on qualitative methods. Feminist Theory, 10(3), 295-308.

About the Author

Trisha Gentle, EdD has dedicated her life over the past thirty years to the efforts of social change. Through her work with domestic violence, sexual assault, trafficking, and survivors of homicide, she has provided leadership and development for a wide range of programs, departments, and agencies. She possesses extensive experience in program development, strategic planning, financial oversite, legislative change, and full system training. This experience has been gained through her positions leading community-based organizations, governmental departments within public safety, and providing consulting to entities local, national, and international. Dr. Gentle's passion has been and remains in ending oppression in all its forms and in addressing the impact of oppression within the lives of individuals and within the criminal and social justice systems of society at large. She is a graduate of Fielding Graduate University, with a doctorate in education. Dr. Gentle may be contacted at tgentle55@gmail.com.

CHAPTER 4

EMPLOYEE-BUILT ORGANIZATIONAL RESILIENCE CAPACITY: GETTING TO SPECIFIC BELIEFS AND BEHAVIORS

Marie Sonnet, PhD
Fellow, Institute for Social Innovation, Fielding Graduate University
Owner and Principal, Sonnet Organization Consulting

Abstract

Amid seemingly incessant turbulence, a targeted organizational focus on creating an employee-built, behavior-based capacity for resilience is a desirable and practical readiness strategy. In this chapter, the author asserts that as employees work together with specific beliefs and behaviors in use, they create a reliable storehouse of capabilities that can be applied across dynamic circumstances, planned and unplanned, generating a strategic change advantage. To accomplish this, though, scholars, consultants, and managers need to move beyond the general recommendations of organizational resilience models to the specifics of what one would assess and develop with employees to generate a robust capacity for collective resilience, answering *"Where are we now and on what exactly should we focus?"* Using an inductive research process and a scale development protocol, the author identifies beliefs and behaviors present when an organization responds to change and adversity with resilience. These items can then be tested, refined, and used as an instrument for assessment and development of a workgroup-based capacity for resilience. This effort responds to the need in the literature and in practice to define a resilience management strategy that makes operational resilience a "repeatable, predictable, manageable, and improvable process" (Annarelli & Nonino, 2016, p. 10).

Keywords: organizational resilience, change readiness, innovation, employee-built capacity, organizational change, strategic change capability, strategic human resource management

Fostering a Resilient Response Capability in an Organizational System

Organizational resilience can be conceptualized as a collective response to change and adversity that not only sustains core characteristics and functions under pressure but innovates to meet situational demands, generating more shared learning as a resource. It's a consequential capability in volatile environments that, quite surprisingly, can be left to chance. That is, we assume it's present or don't pay much attention to it until it is tested. As an underutilized asset, organizations raise risk exposure and the avoidable costs of change. It is proposed that those who pay attention to deliberately building a *capacity* for a resilient response as a readiness strategy have a strategic advantage. Like a bank asset, there is a reserve of resilience capacity built up as employees work together in a resilience-building environment. It is the purpose of this paper to identify what specifically employees do that contributes to a vault of valuable, resilience-ready capabilities so that those collective characteristics can be better studied and supported in vital organizations.

The first task will be to acknowledge the complexity of impacting a human system, particularly one under stress, and to recognize the definitional tensions in resilience research along with the impacts of a wide diffusion of interest in resilience. The second task will be to examine Lengnick-Hall, Beck, and Lengnick-Hall's (2011) framework for building organizational resilience capacity and apply Ajzen's (2009) principle of behavior aggregation to suggest that behavioral consistency over time and contexts can accrue to an underlying disposition of resilience capacity. A final task will be to sort through descriptors, antecedents, and enablers in the organizational resilience literature to identify a specific set of employee beliefs and behaviors and propose them as contributing to a ready, reliable organizational capacity for a resilient response generated in a workgroup setting. Such a set can then be further tested.

Acknowledging Complexity

Impacting employee behaviors in an organization is a complex undertaking. In his chapter on organization as flux and transformation, Morgan (2006) described change as an emergent and thus an uncontrollable force. He encouraged new metaphors for the organization, such as a complex adaptive system (Holland, 1995), to identify what could better facilitate an organization's response to change. For example, managers could create contexts and conditions wherein employees self-organize to respond to the uncertainties of change that can't be scripted in advance. Other metaphors followed from Holling's (1973) work in ecological systems. One is the organization as a socio-ecological system (Berkes, Folke, & Colding, 2000; Folke, 2006, 2016) where "humans in nature" (Folke, 2006, p. 261) create a critical interplay between social dynamics and ecosystem development. Others include the organization as a member of a larger, emergent, networked system of actors (Mars, Bronstein, & Lusch, 2014) and the organization as a human social system (Fath, Dean, & Katzmair, 2015).

To impact change readiness, these ways of viewing an organization are useful. Fath et al. (2015) identified human systems' advantages that don't exist in even complex biological ecosystems. These include the potential for responsive dynamic preparedness and management as well as the abilities to activate energy and grow, to self-organize to store information and capital, to improvise to maintain function; and to learn, forgive, and let go in order to reorient. Human systems also have the ability to recover from surprise and "to have the capability, *in*

135

advance, to handle classes of surprises or challenges" (Woods, 2015, p. 3).

The leap from biological adaptability to human systems' adaptability, however, creates a clash between complex adaptive system frameworks of emergent properties and social science system frameworks of intentional behavior (Hahn & Nykvist, 2017). Hahn and Nykvist (2017) described a recent shift to research of resilience in social-ecological systems that have intentional agents, power dynamics, and conflicts and where norms and even facts reflect preferences. Who is setting the goals? Interpreting the information? Different interests, values, and objectives of actors in a human-social system can even lead to perverse resilience (Phelan, Henderson-Sellers, & Taplin, 2013) where "resilience within a system is undesirable to the extent that it is socially unjust, inconsistent with ecosystem health or threatens overall system viability" (p. 8).

Human agency, then, adds a less understood and therefore less predictable component to natural systems (Fath, et al., 2015). Unlike species in biological ecosystems, organizational leaders have the potential to forecast future conditions and create strategies and structures designed to decrease risk and uncertainty, but there is no guarantee that such proactive planning will prevent degradation (Mars et al., 2014). Organizations can even undermine their own sources of preparedness as they make tradeoffs or miss how employees are making up for adaptive shortfalls (Folke, 2006).

With the nature of no guarantees in mind, the forecasts of future conditions are sobering. They are for more change and faster change. Futurist and Distinguished Fellow at the Institute for the Future, Bob Johansen (2017) advised leaders to adopt new literacies now to handle the increasing speed, frequency, scope, and scale of disruption and what he called "explosive connectivity" and "asymmetric upheaval" that will create a disruptive, "distributed everything" (p. 13). We are urged both to act now and to get ready to act. Readiness applies personally to leaders, as Johansen (2017) advises, but it can also be examined as a multi-level construct (Rafferty, Jimmieson, & Armenakis, 2013) – the individual, workgroup, and organizational capacity to undertake change and to manage it as a strategic ability to constantly adapt to the environment. In the midst of acknowledged complexity, a pursuit of collective resilience as a multi-level construct is an imperative for managing risk (van de Vegt. Essens, Walström, & George, 2015).

Navigating planned change and surprise change

In the readiness literature, the referent change is a specific, planned change. Change readiness in this circumstance is described as a "comprehensive attitude" (Holt, Armenakis, Feild, & Harris, 2007, p. 235) that is a function of what is being changed, how the change is being implemented, the circumstances under which the change is occurring, and the characteristics of individuals being asked to change. A net set of beliefs about the planned change is generated that promotes either resistance or adoptive behaviors. Scaccia et al. (2015) described the necessary components of readiness for a planned change as: 1) motivation for the change (beliefs and perspectives about the need for the change and its likelihood for success), 2) the innovation-specific capabilities needed to implement the change with quality, and 3) general organizational capacities like structure, resources, and demonstrable management support needed to maintain a functioning and even innovating organization. It is proposed here that resilience is an important organizational capacity. Scaccia et al. (2015) maintained that readiness varies as these components vary, making it a developable asset.

We must also build an organizational readiness for surprise – for unexpected, unplanned change or adversity that Johansen (2017) described as the new normal. The organizational capacity needed for that challenge is also resilience, specifically a stored capacity for resilience. This capacity comprises employee-built capabilities that supply a strategic readiness resource for recovery, shared learning, and inventiveness in times of volatility, surprise, complexity, and threat – capabilities hard to create in the moment. They are best built over time as employees work together in an environment that supports their development. Incidents of planned change can be laboratories for their development.

A focus on preparing for surprise echoes Scaccia et al.'s (2015) pursuit of innovation readiness components. They advise targeting beliefs, capabilities, and organizational support. The practitioner, of course, needs to know which beliefs and behaviors management should support to build the needed resilience capabilities – the goal of this chapter. One source for these elements are prior incidents of handling surprise. Woods' (2015) asserted that it is possible to engineer resilience into diverse systems and networks by "finding, studying, and modeling the biological and human systems that are prepared to handle surprises" (p. 4). We'll consider organizational resilience literature that supplies such information.

Grappling with the Concept of Organizational Resilience

Across the ecological metaphors of organization, resilience is a common characteristic and so are its inherent tensions. For example, Folke (2006) defined resilience as the capacity of a system to absorb and reorganize to both retain essentially the same characteristics and functions *and* to self-reorganize structures and processes for renewal and invention. He called this "an interplay between sustaining and developing with change" (p. 259). Resilience generates adaptive capacity so that the system can withstand disturbance and retain function while self-organizing to learn, transform, and innovate. Folke (2006) defined adaptability as the capacity of people to build resilience through collective action. He defined transformability as the capacity of people to create a fundamentally new social–ecological system when ecological, political, social, or economic conditions make the existing system untenable.

In organizational resilience literature, there is a waning definitional tension between resilience as recovery or "bounce back" in the engineering sense of elasticity and resilience as renewal or reinvention to meet new conditions. Aldunce, Beilin, Handmer, & Howden (2014) argued that "bouncing back" would place the system in the same risk as if it were a closed system. Instead, a system can learn and reorganize while retaining identifying functions. Fath et al. (2015) summarized that resilience is the capacity, indeed the intentional capacity, to successfully navigate all stages of the complex adaptive cycle: growth, development, survival, and renewal.

Another kind of tension results from the variety of research perspectives in organizational resilience study. This is captured well by Linnenluecke's (2017) review of resilience in business and management research in which she describes a growing body of literature from 1977 to 2014 yielding five distinct research threads: 1) organizational responses to external threats, 2) organizational reliability, 3) employee strengths, 4) the adaptability of business models, and 5) design principles that reduce supply chain vulnerabilities and disruptions. Linnenluecke noted that each research thread can present its own definition and operationalization of resilience.

One can add applications of organizational resilience. In her review, Sonnet (2016) found that provocative polarities described organizational resilience (see Table 1.) Acknowledging and engaging with seemingly opposite dynamics can help to understand and foster collective resilience in practice.

Addressing Risks of the Diffusion of Resilience as a Desirable Goal
There has been an "explosion" (Folke, 2016, p. 44) of academic literature about organizational resilience) and the term "resilient" is widely adopted in popular parlance as an explanatory concept, a desirable trait, and a descriptive term. Along with ubiquity comes

risks of overadoption (Rogers, 2003) that could render the pursuit of an organizational characteristic like resilience meaningless or rote. Love and Cebon (2008) described how imitation, theorization, and institutionalization by "knowledge entrepreneurs" (p. 245) that include academics, consultants, and authors can have a "homogenizing influence" (p. 244) that accelerates diffusion but presses out distinction among firms. Later adoption of resilience initiatives may be more for legitimacy reasons rather than for an important connection with organizational meaning and values. The practitioner is wise to assess that connection and strengthen it.

Table 1. *Polarities Describing Organizational Resilience*

Polarities describing organizational resilience	
• A latent capacity and an active response	• Pursuing core stability and constant improvement
• An individual and a collective response	• Involving centralization and decentralization
• Employing art and engineering	• Requiring trust and skepticism
• Consisting of enablers and outcomes	• Involving recovery and innovation
• An unmitigated good and a political creation	• Requiring planning and adaptation
• A practiced and an invented approach	• A capacity and a capability
• A fixed trait and an ongoing developmental process	• A potential energy and a kinetic energy

One strategy is to recognize resilience as a dynamic, strategic capability (Teece, Pisano, & Schuen, 1997) embedded in an organization so that it is generic to other capabilities. For example, resilience can be considered generic to the organizational change capability essential for an organization to operate as dynamically stable (McGuinness & Morgan, 2005; Oxtoby, McGuinness, & Morgan, 2002). It is generic to sustainability, adaptability, and transformability (Folke et al., 2016) and to the strategic agility that enables an organization to make quick, decisive, effective moves as it anticipates, initiates, and takes advantage of change (Lengneck-Hall & Beck, 2009). It is generic to high-reliability organizations (Weick, Sutcliffe, and Obtsfeld, 2008) and to product innovation (Akgün & Keskin, 2014). In other words, building a collective capacity for resilience is not a fad but the development of a core competence.

Selecting a Definition in Use

Finally, one must take a definitional position. In her review of definitions of organizational resilience, Sonnet (2016) found a central polarity. The dominant group contained those definitions that convey organizational resilience as an outcome or an expended resource; that is, how did the organization adapt (or not) after an event? How well *did* we do? Langedec (1993) referred to this circumstance as an "abrupt and brutal audit. At a moment's notice, everything that was left unprepared becomes a complex problem and every weakness comes rushing to the forefront" (p. 54). Existing strengths can become apparent, too.

A smaller group of definitions included the *capacity* to respond. How well *will* we do? This category represents the potential energy of a latent readiness response containing practiced beliefs and behaviors associated with resilience capabilities. For developing resilience capacity as a collection of ready capabilities, Vogus and Sutcliffe's (2007) definition of resilience is most relevant – "To be resilient is to be vitally prepared" (p. 3418). This is the definition in use here as change and adversity are "inherently future focused and a focus on capacity is potentially more valuable than a focus on outcomes" (John Austin, PhD, personal correspondence, October 2018). Of course, the polarity of preparation and response requires that both be activated in a developmental process that involves real time assessing and flexing with different solution sets.

For research purposes, Cho, Mathiassen, and Robey (2007) recommended that resilience be viewed as a process capability or potential separate from the active, adaptive phase. They gave these reasons: 1) resilience consists of multiple capabilities, some of which may not be possessed by an organization; 2) specific capabilities may be effective in overcoming specific barriers to change, and 3) a resilience capability may be related to both successful and unsuccessful adoption behaviors. The capabilities that accrue to a collective resilience capacity are the focus of this chapter.

Building a Collective Resilience Capacity
A Promising Conceptual Framework

Having wrestled with the complexity and tensions associated with organizational resilience in order to identify a meaningful approach, we can look for a promising conceptual framework. The work of Lengnick-Hall and Beck (2005, 2009) and Lengnick-Hall et al. (2011) offer a theoretical and practical contribution for building collective resilience in an organization. They maintained that there are three component properties to resilience capacity: cognitive resilience, behavioral resilience, and contextual resilience.

Cognitive resilience includes noticing, interpreting, analyzing, and formulating responses with ingenuity and new skill development. This includes constructive sensemaking in unfamiliar situations where interpretations and judgments are required as well as a strong, value-driven core identity that offers a prime directive for making choices.

Behavioral resilience is the "engine that moves an organization forward" (Lengnick-Hall & Beck, 2005, p. 751). This includes a complex and varied action inventory (as yet unspecified) that gives an organization more choices – a toolkit for action – particularly in new circumstances. Here, functional habits described as rehearsed routines automatically open communication channels, create interpersonal ties, and seek multiple sources of information. Habits of continuous dialogue help construct meaning and direction in ambiguous circumstances.

Contextual resilience provides the setting where cognitive and behavioral resilience can flourish. It includes deep social capital that evolves from repeated personal interactions over time between people and between organizations that are based on trust. Benefits include access to broader information pools, expanded knowledge and resource sources, and the experience of interdependence, sense of purpose, and meaning in uncertainty. Broad networks that yield resources, concessions, and assistance when needed are a component of contextual resilience. These introduce requisite variety and diversity into an organization when adaptation and innovation are required.

Of course, employees, not the anthropomorphic "organization", build the system response. They are enacting and activating the specific resource-building responses of all three components in daily collaborations with one another. "An organization's capacity for resilience is a multilevel collective attribute emerging from the capabilities, actions, and interactions of individuals and units within the firm" (Lengnick-Hall et al., 2011, p. 253). Management can specifically develop capabilities, routines, practices, and processes to support these interactions. The framework proposed by Lengnick-Hall et al. (2011) identified a provocative set of employee "contributions" available in a resilient organization. These are shown in Table 2 as they are listed by Lengnick-Hall et al. in the cognitive, behavioral, and contextual dimensions. The authors then presented strategic human resource principles and policies that would support these contributions. While this framework has two particular weaknesses to be discussed here, it offers an actionable focus on the components of an employee-built collective resilience capacity. Employee "contributions" are examples of behavioral guidelines that serve as inputs to a set of specific behaviors proposed in this chapter.

One weakness of Lengnick-Hall et al.'s (2011) framework is that some employee contributions are still too broad or generally stated for targeted impact. In observable, behavioral terms, we want to know more specifically for each component what to observe, assess, enhance, and support. Also, the items in list as presented cannot be tested for their relationship to an underlying variable, organizational resilience capacity. This chapter proposes that a specific list of beliefs and behaviors particularly active in the workgroup setting is a next step in framework development.

Table 2

Desired Employee Contributions According to Framework by Lengnick-Hall et al., 2011

Desired employee contributions by dimension of organizational resilience[a]		
Cognitive dimension	Behavioral dimension	Contextual dimension
Expertise	Devising unconventional, yet robust responses to unprecedented challenges	Developing interpersonal connections and resource supply lines that lead to the ability to act quickly
Opportunism		
Creativity	Combining originality and initiative to capitalize on an immediate situation	
Decisiveness despite uncertainty		
Questioning fundamental assumptions	Sometimes following a dramatically different course of action from that which is the norm for the organization	Sharing information and knowledge widely
Conceptualizing solutions that are novel and appropriate	Practicing repetitive, over-learned routines that provide the first response to any unexpected threat	Sharing power and accountability
	Taking actions and making investments before they are needed to ensure that an organization is able to benefit from situations that emerge	

Note. [a]From Lengnick-Hall et al. (2011), p. 249.

A second weakness is the reliance by Lengnick-Hall et al. (2011) on strategic human resource management to develop these capabilities. The field of strategic human resource management is examining gaps between its aspirations and achievements (Jackson, Shulyers, & Jiang, 2014) and renewing its search for managerial insights about how to create and capture organizational value (Markoulli, Lee, Byington, & Felps, 2016). As an indication of its impact, the role that human resource personnel took in a change initiative (administrative experts vs. strategic change agents) had a significant impact on employee expectations for the success of an organizational change (Brown, Kulik,

Cregan, & Metz, 2017). We may not yet know how to deploy human resource personnel in support of resilience readiness capabilities.

A Behavioral Model of Organizational Resilience Capacity

Instead of relying on one department, what is needed is a broader managerial ownership of organizational resilience capacity, including human resource leaders, to create the vital conditions in an organization that foster desired employee beliefs and behaviors. Figure 1 presents a behavioral model of organizational resilience capacity (adapted from Sonnet, 2016) that requires involvement of all organizational stakeholders. There are improvement science processes to help stakeholders examine, prioritize, and align inducements, routines and practices, cultural norms, and individual resilience to support collective resilience capacity beliefs and behaviors. Alternatively, benign neglect can foster the unintended deterrence of resilience capacity, the expectation that employees just have "it", or the reliance on superhero performance in high stakes situations. These outcomes increase organizational risk.

Figure 1. A behavioral model of organizational resilience capacity adapted from Sonnet (2016).

The Aggregation of Behavior

How can employee behaviors, supported by vital conditions, result in an organizational attribute? Lengnick-Hall et al. (2011) described a process by which "employee attitudes and behaviors ...become shared over time" and "in the aggregate" (p. 251) increase the organization's capacity for resilience. Their reference to the aggregation of behavior prompts a referral to Ajzen (2009) for an understanding of this process. Ajzen asserted that attitudes (dispositions to respond favorably or unfavorably to an object, person, institution, or event) and personality traits (characteristics that have a pervasive influence on responses) do predict behavior. Attitudes and traits, though, are "latent and hypothetical" (p. 2) and knowable only through observable, overt actions, expressed behavioral intentions, verbal statements regarding behavior, and nonverbal cues. Even so, Ajzen stated, they are relatively enduring dispositions that cohere around thoughts, feelings, and actions (the tripartite model of attitude, Breckler, 1984). "This dispositional view implies *behavioral consistency*; that is, consistency among different behaviors, performed in different situations, so long as the behaviors in question are all instances of the same underlying disposition" (Ajzen, 2009, p. 31).

Given Ajzen's (2009) premise, the researcher can assert that a collective, underlying disposition of resilience produces consistency in the behaviors of an organization's employees – a desirable state. As a caution, Ajzen underscored little consistency between single actions and he noted a persistent inability to predict specific behaviors. He observed that what is more promising is to consider behavioral tendencies and to aggregate observations made on different occasions and in different contexts using multiple-act aggregates that reflect the broad response disposition in question. Building on this principle of aggregation, it proposed here that an instrument design strategy could be used to identify stable behavioral tendencies. There is "evidence for consistency between behavioral measures that aggregate across

146

different actions, so long as each aggregate assesses the same broad underlying disposition" (Ajzen, 2009, p. 143). In the language of scale development, the broad underlying disposition is the latent variable to be assessed (Hinkin, 1998). In this case, the latent variable is organizational resilience capacity.

Lengnick-Hall et al. (2011) proposed that the aggregation of certain employee behaviors describes a collective resilient response capacity. If organizational resilience can be characterized as a broad response disposition, which is a collection of behavioral tendencies reflected by multiple acts performed on different occasions and in different contexts, the reported presence of those acts could be aggregated to a consistent collective behavior of resilience that can be assessed and strengthened. The premise of this chapter is that identifying which behaviors accrue to a resilient response is foundational to building organizational resilience capacity.

It is also claimed here that resilience-building in an organization is the result of people working together. Tillement, Cholez, and Reverdy (2009) questioned whether resilience can even be attributed to an organization as a whole or whether it rests solely with intra- and inter-group dynamics. Lengnick-Hall et al. (2011) acknowledged the importance of dynamics such as system/subsystem interactions, complex social networks, and actions and interaction effects in a collective structure, and advocated a focus on "how individuals collectively enable the organization to be resilient" (p. 245). They asserted that, in the social organization, this happens in the context of those with whom individuals work most often. Sonnet (2016) suggested that once a set of beliefs and behaviors proposed to aggregate to a collective resilience capacity is identified, that capacity could be assessed using an individual level of analysis but with a social, work group frame of reference ("In my work group, we...") to query the presence of specific beliefs and behaviors associated with organizational resilience capacity. Identifying those is the next task.

Beliefs and Behaviors Associated with Organizational
Resilience Capacity

Woods (2015) noted a "resilience paradox' where the ability of systems to be adaptive in the future is measured by data on how the system has adapted in the past. As case studies reveal, that learning is limited by how situations can appear structured *after the fact* (Sutcliffe, 2005). Resilience can also be interpreted with retrospective sensemaking for more self-serving purposes, creating a myth of resilience subject to manipulation (Kuhlicke, 2013). With these limitations in mind, learning from past performance contributes to understanding the fundamental properties of networks, systems, and organizations able to build, modify, and sustain effective adaptive capacities.

To expose these capacities, three strategies were employed in an inductive study: 1) examine data across case studies in the literature, 2) consider theoretical models offered to explain resilience dynamics, and 3) review measurement tools proposed by researchers. The goal was to extract specific actions attributed to a collective resilient response. Table 3 presents core sources from the literature.

See next page for Tables

148

Table 3

Core Sources of Employee Behaviors Associated with
Organizational Resilience Capacity

Studies of organizational experience	Theoretical models examining organizational resilience	Tools proposed for assessing organizational resilience capacity
Beunza, D., & Stark, D. (2003). The organization of responsiveness: Innovation and recovery in the trading rooms of Lower Manhattan. *Socio-Economic Review, 1*(2), 135-164.	Baker, T., Miner, A. S., & Eesley, D. T. (2003). Improvising firms: Bricolage, account giving and improvisational competencies in the founding process. *Research Policy, 32*(2), 255-276.	Horne, J.F., III & J.E. Orr. (1998). Assessing behaviors that create resilient organizations. *Employment Relations Today, 24* (4): 29–39.
Cho, S., Mathiassen, L., & Robey, D. (2007). Dialectics of resilience: a multi-level analysis of a telehealth innovation. *Journal of Information Technology, 22*(1), 24-35.	Braithwaite, J., Wears, R. L., Hollnagel, E. (2015). Resilient health care: Turning patient safety on its head. *International Journal for Quality in Health Care, 27*(5), 418–420.	Kantur, D., & Iseri-Say, A. I. (2015). Measuring organizational resilience: A scale development. *Journal of Business Economics and Finance, 4*(3), 456-472.
Freeman, S. F., Hirschhorn, L., & Maltz, M. (2004). The power of moral purpose: Sandler O'Neill & Partners in the aftermath of September 11th, 2001. *Organization Development Journal, 22*(4), 69.	Gibson, C. A., & Tarrant, M. (2010). A 'conceptual models' approach to organisational resilience. *Australian Journal of Emergency Management, 25*(2), 6.	Lee, A., Vargo, J. & Seville, E. (2013). Developing a tool to measure and compare organizations' resilience. *Natural Hazards Review, 14*, 29-41.
Gittell, J. H., Cameron, K., Lim, S., & Rivas, V. (2006). Relationships, layoffs, and organizational resilience: Airline industry responses to September 11. *The Journal of Applied Behavioral Science, 42*(3), 300-329.	Lengnick-Hall, C. A., Beck, T. E., & Lengnick-Hall, M. L. (2011). Developing a capacity for organizational resilience through strategic human resource management. *Human Resource Management Review, 21*(3), 243-255.	Mallak, L. A. (1998). Measuring resilience in health care provider organizations. *Health Manpower Management, 24*(4), 148-152.
Kayes, D. C. (2004). The 1996 Mount Everest climbing disaster: The breakdown of learning in teams. *Human Relations, 57*(10), 1263-1284.	Mallak, L. A. (1999). Toward a theory of organizational resilience. *Proceedings of the Portland International Conference on Management of Engineering and Technology (PICMET) 1999*, 223.	Mallak, L. A., & Yildiz, M. (2016). Developing a workplace resilience instrument, *Work, 54*(2), 241-253.

Table 3 *continued*
Core Sources of Employee Behaviors Associated with
Organizational Resilience Capacity

Studies of organizational experience	Theoretical models examining organizational resilience	Tools proposed for assessing organizational resilience capacity
Meyer, A. D. (1982). Adapting to environmental jolts. *Administrative Science Quarterly, 27*, 515-537.	Weick, K. E. (1988). Enacted sensemaking in crisis situations [1]. *Journal of Management studies, 25*(4), 305-317.	Stephenson, A., Vargo, J., & Seville, E. (2010). Measuring and comparing organisational resilience in Auckland. *Australian Journal of Emergency Management, The, 25*(2), 27.
Weick, K. E. (1990). The vulnerable system: An analysis of the Tenerife air disaster. *Journal of Management, 16*(3), 571-593.	Weick, K. E., Sutcliffe, K. M., & Obstfeld, D. (2008). Organizing for high reliability: Processes of collective mindfulness. *Crisis Management, 3*(1), 81-123.	
Weick, K. E. (1993). The collapse of sensemaking in organizations: The Mann Gulch disaster. *Administrative Science Quarterly*, 628-652	Weick, K. E., & Sutcliffe, K. M. (2011). *Managing the unexpected: Resilient performance in an age of uncertainty* (Vol. 8). John Wiley & Sons.	
Weick, K. E. (2010). Reflections on enacted sensemaking in the Bhopal disaster. *Journal of Management Studies, 47*(3), 537-550.		

Separating Descriptors, Enablers, and Antecedents from Desired Behaviors

In the process of searching the literature for specific beliefs and behaviors associated with an employee-built organizational resilience capacity, the author found that descriptors, antecedents, and enablers of behaviors were often used in place of specific employee behaviors. This condition presents at least four risks: conflating the level of analysis for the researcher, encumbering the practitioner with a generalized fix before the targeted behavior is understood, jeopardizing resilience improvement initiatives with diffuse and likely unmeasurable objectives; and, hindering the valid assessment of employee-built organizational resilience capacity such that strengths and vulnerabilities cannot be recognized. Still, these studies and articles can be mined for their underlying beliefs and behaviors.

Sections of Table 4 present found descriptors, enablers, and antecedents in three suggested groups: 4a) work environment, 4b) job design, and 4c) management. A next step is to examine these for a proposed set of specific employee beliefs and behaviors that can be further tested.

Table 4a

Descriptors, Enablers, and Antecedents of Employee-built Organizational Resilience Capacity – Work Environment

Work environment descriptors, enablers, and antecedents			
Members have an organizational identity.	Members have a strong sense of purpose. More than a statement, purpose is enacted through the collective assumptions made by participants about the consequences of their activities.	There is collective sensemaking. "To deal with ambiguity, interdependent people search for meaning, settle for plausibility, and move on…People are socialized to make do, be resilient, treat constraints as self-imposed, strive for plausibility, keep showing up, use retrospect to get a sense of direction, and articulate descriptions that energize (Weick, Sutcliffe, & Obstfeld, 2005, p. 419)".	There is an accumulation of established and practiced behaviors for innovative problem solving – seeing solutions that are novel yet appropriate.
There is a reservoir of options, a "storehouse" of capabilities (Vogus & Sutcliffe, 2007).	There is a tolerance for ambiguity.	Members persist through disturbance.	Experience develops both expertise (a behavioral repertoire) and confidence (cognitive resilience).
Work environment is conducive to taking interpersonal risks.	There is dispersed influence - individual and group accountability and shared decision-making.	There are "heterarchical rather than hierarchical structures" that allow for self-organization, lateral coordination, and distributed intelligence (Beunza & Stark, 2002).	There are authentic core values.
Ingenuity, inventiveness, and bricolage are valued.	Expertise is valued.	Tenacity is valued.	There is deep social capital marked by respectful interactions – face to face, ongoing dialogues rooted in trust, honesty, and self-respect.

Table 4b

Descriptors, Enablers, and Antecedents of Employee-built
Organizational Resilience Capacity – Job Design

Job design descriptors, enablers, and antecedents		
Members are alert to evolving circumstances. They have a rich awareness of detail. They "continually track small failures, resist oversimplification, remain sensitive to operations, maintain capabilities for resilience, and take advantage of shifting locations of expertise (Weick & Sutcliffe, 2007, p. 2)".	Members practice routines and activities to develop useful habits and practiced resourcefulness. Routines are action patterns that summarize knowledge and experience. Three routines "to absorb complexity": 1) routines to create plans that are malleable and sufficiently general that they can be used in a variety of situations, 2) routines to notice exceptions and unexpected events, and 3) routines that prevent imposition of a ready-made structure on decisions (Lengnick-Hall & Beck, 2005, p. 745).	Members have useful habits – well-rehearsed routines, emerging from core values, which provide a first response to a threat that generates options rather than constraints.
Members have formed broad resource networks – relationships with others who could share key resources – suppliers, valued customers, and strategic partners. This creates slack and an action inventory as well as social capital beyond firm's boundaries. "Relational reserves" are a source of resilience (Gittell et al., 2006).	Members display wisdom – a blend of caution and confidence, skepticism and curiosity – a disregard for precedent.	Members use lessons from their own and others' experiences to better manage prevailing circumstances. They can learn and apply lessons in real time as these emerge.
Resourcefulness includes questioning precedent, status quo, and norms.	Each member has discretion and responsibility for attaining the organization's interests.	

152

Table 4c

*Descriptors, Enablers, and Antecedents of Employee-built
Organizational Resilience Capacity – Management*

Management descriptors, enablers, and antecedents				
fers a genuine vision lear vision and goals…well-understood and communicated throughout the organization (Seville et al., 2006)."	Takes action and makes investments before they are needed to ensure that the organization is able to benefit from situations that emerge.	Enables members to deliberately unlearn or discard behaviors that lead to inappropriate constraints.	Fosters attitudes and behaviors that promote a collaborative response to complexities.	Fosters useful that includ habits of investigati rather than assumptio collaborati rather than antagonisn flexibility 1 than rigidit
sters use of language that frames conditions as opportunities for problem solving and action.	Provides access to resources and financial reserves.	Provides minimum specifications to allow for local design.	Enables members to see their work as part of a larger "role system" and to flex across roles when necessary.	Values preparedn•
es vocabulary to convey a clear sense of direction, constructs meaning, describes situations; implies meaning and emotion as well as capability, influence, competence, and consistent core values.	Creates a "mindful infrastructure… built out of a broad repertoire of action and experience, the ability to recombine fragments of past experience into novel responses, emotional control, skill at successful interaction, and knowledge of how the system functions (Weick & Sutcliffe, 2007 p. 3)."	Ensures members have resources to take business advantage of situations as they arise.	Generates emergent leadership (often from the middle) that provides direction in times of high uncertainty. Applies capabilities and unifies the operation of processes, resources, infrastructure, technology, information, and knowledge.	Develops tools technology "team play designed to function as cooperativ partners (Christoffe & Woods, 2002).
ables members to form long-term partnerships and cross-functional collaborations. There are bridges across conventional boundaries.	Prepares members to take advantage of situations; investments have been made to allow for mining opportunities.			

Getting to Beliefs and Behaviors

The goal of this study was to identify specific beliefs and behaviors associated with an employee-built organizational resilience capacity so that they can be examined and acted upon. Two steps were taken. Based on the findings in Table 4, a list of resulting belief and behavioral

153

statements was generated. These are shown in Table 5. These statements were then refined using item-creation techniques for scale development.

Table 5

Resulting Beliefs and Behaviors Proposed as Associated with Employee-Built Organizational Resilience Capacity

Resulting employee beliefs and behaviors		
Employees talk with confidence that they can meet a challenge. "We can do it!"	Employees are keenly aware of small changes in circumstances that could indicate bigger threats or opportunities.	Employees talk about conditions as opportunities for problem solving and action.
Employees use shared stories and experiences to solve new problems.	Employees analyze and interpret evolving situations.	Employees practice investigating rather that assuming.
Employees speak up about what they know.	Employees have strong relationships with others who could share key resources.	Employees have formed long-term, cross-functional partnerships.
Employees who have expertise about a topic are consulted during decision-making regardless of their title.	Employees decide on an action and pursue it.	Employees work to minimum specifications, so they can customize for local conditions.
Employees as individuals and groups are accountable for achieving outcomes.	Employees make plans that are flexible enough to be adapted to a variety of situations.	Employees know how the work system functions as a whole to get things done.
Employees share information needed to solve problems across departments.	Employees challenge the way things were done before.	Employees clearly picture where their role fits in the larger work system.
Employee choices reflect the values of the company, top to bottom, in a real and genuine way.	Employees are resourceful, making do with what they have in novel situations.	Employees know other roles and can step in if needed.
Employees have face-to-face interactions that are honest.	Employees are skeptical about ready-made answers, preferring to ask questions before committing to a response.	Employees discard behaviors if they create constraints not helpful to the situation.
Employees have ongoing dialogues that are rooted in trust and respect.	Employees generate options for response to a situation.	Employees step up to provide direction, especially in times of high uncertainty, no matter their title.
Employees practice to develop useful habits and routines.	Employees look for solutions as a first response rather than detailing constraints or blame.	Employees use tools and technology that have been developed to be part of the team response.
	Employees place a high value on being ready for change.	

For use in observation, assessment, and development of collective conduct, the resulting statements in Table 5 are still too broad to be tested. The principles of item generation for a scale (DeVellis, 2012) were used to provide guidance for their refinement. These include clarity of expression, brevity, reading level, concept singularity, and attention to grammatical construction.

Using these guidelines, a set of items representing the proposed beliefs and behaviors associated with employee-built organizational resilience capacity were developed and presented to a set of experts working on the topic of resilience. These experts were asked to critique items for relevance, ambiguity, problem wording, conciseness, and missing elements. In a facilitated session, items were also presented to a group of typical employee respondents with backgrounds in different organizations. Observations were made about interpretation, speed of response, questions asked, and agreement of meaning. These reviews helped to develop content validity.

This process generated 42 items. Table 6 shows the items sorted into initial hypothesized factors. These items could then be administered in a survey format using the stem "In my workgroup, we…" Resulting data could be analyzed using statistical techniques for scale development (DeVellis, 2012). The goals would be to validate that these statements describe a common latent variable, remove items that aren't statistically related, identify resulting factors that organize the items, and create an organizational resilience capacity scale that could be repeatedly tested and refined. The result could give practitioners a needed evidence base for reliably assessing and improving collective resilience capacity in the context of their work environment.

Table 6

For Study, Employee Beliefs and Behaviors Associated with a Collective Capacity for Resilience

Communication (7)	Mission (7)	Resources (8)	Ownership (6)	Skepticism (6)	Norms (8)
Talk together to make sense of situations as they are happening	Use the values of the company to guide our actions in a real and genuine way	Figure how to fix things using what we have on hand	X Rely on our experience about how best to do the work	X Question the way things were done before	Find possibility in most all circumstances
Have face to face conversations that are honest	Know how our jobs fit in the big picture of how work gets done	Get materials and equipment from multiple sources	Adjust how we do our work based on the actual situation	Try out our ideas to learn from what does and doesn't work	Are ready for anything that comes our way
Tell stories about times we solved problems together	Are able to state what our business is about in 3-4 sentences	Get reliable information from multiple sources	Call upon employees with needed expertise no matter their title, position, or department	X Look for results that are different than what we expected	Value the past experience of employees
X Find something to laugh about in even difficult situations	Practice what we would do as a first response to the unexpected	Know which company employees have what expertise	Stick with what we are doing until it is done right	X Are able to act when we don't have a clear answer	X Are obsessed with catching errors
Share what we know	X Truly believe that our company does important work	Have a working knowledge of each other's jobs	Follow a set of SOPs when dealing with unusual situations	X Worry about making a mistake	Look for explanations first rather than blame
Talk about what we've learned on the job	X Stop doing something when we see it's not working	Use bits of past experience to come up with new ideas	Take ownership of what needs to be done	X Ask questions rather than assume we already know	X Act without permission
Stay in constant communication	Get to do what we do best	X Can depend on other depts or units for help			Would rather fix a problem than complain about it
		Cultivate valuable partnerships with people outside the company			Just know "We can do it!"

Note: Items are sorted into hypothesized factors and assume the stem "In my work group, we…". Items marked by "X" were not retained (Sonnet, 2016).

Discussion

In a climate of rapid change and unexpected challenges, post-action analysis of organizational readiness for change and adversity is not enough. Woods (2015) described the challenge this way. "It is not what happens after a surprise that affects the ability to recover; it is what capacities are present before the surprise that can be deployed or mobilized to deal with the surprise" (p. 2). This chapter recommended a proactive approach – deliberately cultivating an employee-built organizational capacity for a resilient response. Acting "before the surprise", however, presents several challenges we are not yet able to meet. How strong is our collective capacity for resilience now? Which resilience capabilities are already strengths we can leverage? Which ones represent potential risks? What do we do to deliberately foster and support employee-built resilience? Are we actually deterring resilience? To conduct these analyses, we have to get to the components of that capacity.

To that aim, this chapter presented a process used to identify specific beliefs and behaviors characteristic of employees as they work together in an organization capable of a resilient response to constant change, planned and unplanned, and unexpected adversity. Existing models, case studies, and organizational resilience capacity scales yielded helpful descriptors, enablers, and antecedents which were mined for specific beliefs and behaviors to be cultivated as a storehouse of capabilities. These are the building blocks that, with deliberate focus, can aggregate to a persistent collective resilient disposition.

With specific items identified, we can move further away from broad strategies that assume impact but leave the practitioner asking, "Where are we now and on what exactly should we focus?" We take a step towards a more targeted, evidence-based plan to impact readiness for change and surprise. The prospect of data around behavioral items in a specific setting empowers a practitioner who can build a strategy, indeed a business case, to answer the questions posed above. Specific behavioral goals could be identified. Most importantly, organizational leaders could decide to deliberately align cultural norms, routines, practices, and inducements (Figure 1) to support prioritized collective resilience capacity behaviors. Conditions related to job design, management, and work environment (such as those in Table 4) could be selected for joint action based on that prioritization in a local setting. Hopefully, employees are part of the prioritization, design, and implementation processes.

Further Research

It is risky task, indeed, to select finite elements for focus in a complex and unpredictable human social system under stress. To do so requires holding the polarity of both practiced and emergent properties of a resilient organization. The task is further complicated by the limited studies available for source data. What is missing or mistakenly emphasized? In addition, local circumstances and characteristics can impact the desirability of an investment in resilience capacity, which may vary with the business cycle or "system state" (Mamouni Limnios, Mazzarol, Ghadounani, and Schilizzi, 2012). Mamouni Limnios et al. argued that factors like cost and fit create boundary conditions that challenge resilience as simply an unmitigated good. Still, in the face of accelerating uncertainty, it seems extremely valuable to know where to start to build a people-based capacity for planned change and surprise.

Three areas of further research are indicated. First, the list of beliefs and behaviors proposed as describing a latent capacity for organizational or collective resilience must be tested in a variety of organizational settings. In an exploratory study, Sonnet (2016) found that retained items coalesced around factors describing purposeful communication behaviors and confident competence beliefs. Secondly, additional studies of behavior, particularly workgroup behavior, in successful and unsuccessful cases of change response can be developed or examined for further source data on beliefs and behaviors. Thirdly, we need to explore the details of each specific item as they relate to vital conditions in an organization. Once an item is prioritized for action, we can explore what questions, discussions, and actions must follow to reliably impact that belief or behavior in a particular setting.

Organizations are under pressure to adapt and evolve under circumstances of rapid change. At the same time, employee-built collective resilience capacity is an underutilized asset that could reduce risk and lower avoidable costs of change. To leverage this proactive capacity, we need to better understand its dynamics in actionable terms. This chapter proposed specific beliefs and behaviors as building blocks of organizational resilience capacity, extending current models and providing both scholars and practitioners a framework for recognizing and strengthening a potential, indeed remarkable, advantage.

References

Ajzen, I. (2009). *Attitudes, personality, and behavior*. New York, NY: McGraw Hill International.

Akgün, A. E., & Keskin, H. (2014). Organisational resilience capacity and firm product innovativeness and performance. *International Journal of Production Research, 52*(23), 6918-6937. doi.org/10.1080/00207543.2014.910624

Aldunce, P., Beilin, R., Handmer, J., & Howden, M. (2014). Framing disaster resilience: The implications of the diverse conceptualisations of "bouncing back". *Disaster Prevention and Management, 23*(3), 252-270. doi.org/10.1108/DPM-07-2013-0130

Annarelli, A., & Nonino, F. (2016). Strategic and operational management of organizational resilience: Current state of research and future directions. *Omega, 62*, 1-18. doi.org/10.1016/j.omega.2015.08.004

Berkes, F., Folke, C., & Colding, J. (Eds.). (2000). *Linking social and ecological systems: Management practices and social mechanisms for building resilience*. New York: Cambridge University Press.

Beunza, D., & Stark, D. (2003). The organization of responsiveness:

Innovation and recovery in the trading rooms of Lower Manhattan. *Socio-Economic Review, 1*(2), 135-164.

Braithwaite, J., Wears, R. L., Hollnagel, E. (2015). Resilient health care: turning patient safety on its head. *International Journal for Quality in Health Care, 27* (5), p. 418–420. doi.org/10.1093/intqhc/mzv063

Breckler, S. J. (1984). Empirical validation of affect, behavior, and cognition as distinct components of attitude. *Journal of Personality and Social Psychology, 47*(6), 1191. doi:10.1037/0022-3514.47.6.1191

Brown, M., Kulik, C. T., Cregan, C., & Metz, I. (2017). Understanding the change–cynicism cycle: The role of HR. *Human Resource Management, 56*(1), 5-24. doi:10.1002/hrm.21708

Cho, S., Mathiassen, L., & Robey, D. (2007). Dialectics of resilience: a multi-level analysis of a telehealth innovation. *Journal of Information Technology, 22*(1), 24-35. doi:10.1057/palgrave.jit.2000088

Cristoffersen, K., & Woods, D. D. (2002). How to make automated systems team players. *Advances in Human Performance and Cognitive Engineering Research, 2*, 1-12.

DeVellis, R. F. (2012). *Scale development: Theory and applications.* Thousand Oaks, CA: Sage.

Fath, B. D., Dean, C. A., & Katzmair, H. (2015). Navigating the adaptive cycle: an approach to managing the resilience of social systems. *Ecology and Society, 20*(2). doi:10.5751/ES-07467-200224

Folke, C. (2006). Resilience: The emergence of a perspective for social–ecological systems analyses. *Global Environmental Change, 16*(3), 253-267.

Folke, C. (2016). Resilience (Republished). *Ecology and Society, 21*(4), 44. doi.org/10.5751/ES-09088-210444

Folke, C., Biggs, R., Norström, A. V., Reyers, B., & Rockström, J.

(2016). Social-ecological resilience and biosphere-based sustainability science. *Ecology and Society*, *21*(3), 41. doi.org/10.5751/ES-08748-210341

Freeman, S. F., Hirschhorn, L., & Maltz, M. (2004). The power of moral purpose: Sandler O'Neill & Partners in the aftermath of September 11th, 2001. *Organization Development Journal*, *22*(4), 69.

Gibson, C. A., & Tarrant, M. (2010). A 'conceptual models' approach to organisational resilience. *Australian Journal of Emergency Management, 25*(2), 6.

Gittell, J. H., Cameron, K., Lim, S., & Rivas, V. (2006). Relationships, layoffs, and organizational resilience: Airline industry responses to September 11. *The Journal of Applied Behavioral Science, 42*(3), 300-329. doi:10.1177/0021886306286466

Hahn, T., and B. Nykvist. 2017. Are adaptations self-organized, autonomous, and harmonious? Assessing the social–ecological resilience literature. *Ecology and Society, 22*(1):12. doi.org/10.5751/ES-09026-22011

Hinkin, T. R. (1998). A brief tutorial on the development of measures for use in survey questionnaires. *Organizational Research Methods, 1*(1), 104-121.

Holland, J., 1995. *Hidden order: How adaptation builds complexity.* Reading, MA: Addison-Wesley.

Holling, C.S., 1973. Resilience and stability of ecological systems. *Annual Review of Ecology and Systematics 4*, 1–23.

Horne, J.F., III & J.E. Orr. (1998). Assessing behaviors that create resilient organizations. *Employment Relations Today, 24* (4): 29–39.

Holt, D. T., Armenakis, A. A., Feild, H. S., & Harris, S. G. (2007). Readiness for organizational change: The systematic development of a scale. *The Journal of Applied Behavioral Science, 43*(2), 232-255.doi: 10.1177/0021886306295295

161

Jackson, S. E., Schuler, R. S., & Jiang, K. (2014). An aspirational framework for strategic human resource management. *The Academy of Management Annals, 8*(1), 1-56. doi.org/10.1080/19416520.2014.872335

Johansen, B. (2017). *The new leadership literacies: Thriving in a future of extreme disruption and distributed everything.* Oakland, CA: Berrett-Koehler.

Kantur D., & Iseri-Say, A. (2012). Organizational resilience: A conceptual integrative framework. *Journal of Management and Organization, 18*(6), 762-773. doi.org/10.1017/S1833367200000420

Kantur, D., & Iseri-Say, A. (2015). Measuring organizational resilience: a scale development. *Journal of Business Economics and Finance, 4*(3). doi:10.17261/Pressacademia.2015313066

Kayes, D. C. (2004). The 1996 Mount Everest climbing disaster: The breakdown of learning in teams. *Human Relations, 57*(10), 1263-1284. doi:10.1177/0018726704048355

Kendra, J. M., & Wachtendorf, T. (2003). Elements of resilience after the World Trade Center disaster: Reconstituting New York City's Emergency Operations Center. *Disasters, 27*(1), 37-53. doi:10.1111/1467-7717.00218

Kuhlicke, C. (2013). Resilience: A capacity and a myth: Findings from an in-depth case study in disaster management research. *Natural Hazards Review, 67*, 61-76

Lagadec, P. (1993). *Preventing chaos in a crisis: Strategies for prevention, control and damage limitation.* Maidenhead/Berkshire, UK: McGraw-Hill.

Lee, A., Vargo, J. & Seville, E. (2013). Developing a tool to measure and compare organizations' resilience. *Natural Hazards Review, 14*, 29-41.
doi:10.1061/(ASCE)NH.1527-6996.0000075

Lengnick-Hall, C. A., & Beck, T. E. (2005). Adaptive fit versus robust transformation: How organizations respond to environmental change. *Journal of Management, 31*(5), 738-757. doi:10.1177/0149206305279367

Lengnick-Hall, C.A. and Beck, T. E. (2009). Resilience capacity and strategic agility: Prerequisites for thriving in a dynamic environment. In Nemeth, C., Hollnagel, E., and Dekker, S. (Eds.), *Resilience engineering perspectives: Preparation and restoration* (Vol. 2) (pp. 39-70). Aldershot, UK: Ashgate.

Lengnick-Hall, C. A., Beck, T. E., & Lengnick-Hall, M. L. (2011). Developing a capacity for organizational resilience through strategic human resource management. *Human Resource Management Review, 21*(3), 243-255. doi:10.1016/j.hrmr.2010.07.001

Linnenluecke, M. K. (2017). Resilience in business and management research: A review of influential publications and a research agenda. *International Journal of Management Reviews, 19*(1), 4-30. doi:10.1111/ijmr.12076

Love, E. G., & Cebon, P. (2008). Meanings on multiple levels: the influence of field level and organizational level meaning systems on diffusion. *Journal of Management Studies, 45*(2), 239-267. doi:10.1111/j.1467-6486.2007.00739.x

Luthans, F., Vogelgesang, G. R., & Lester, P. B. (2006). Developing the psychological capital of resiliency. *Human Resource Development Review, 5*(1), 25-44. doi.org/10.1177%2F1534484305285335

Mallak, L. A. (1998). Measuring resilience in health care provider organizations. *Health Manpower Management, 24*(4), 148-152. doi:10.1108/09552069810215755

Mallak, L. A. (1999). Toward a theory of organizational resilience. *Proceedings of the Portland International Conference on Management of Engineering and Technology (PICMET) 1999*, p. 223. Obtained from author 12/16/13.

Mallak, L. A., & Yildiz, M. (2016). Developing a workplace resilience instrument. *Work, 54*(2), 241-253. doi:10.3233/WOR-162297

Markoulli, M., Lee, C. I., Byington, E., & Felps, W. A. (2017). Mapping human resource management: Reviewing the field and charting future directions. *Human Resource Management Review*, *27*(3), 367-396. doi.org/10.1016/j.hrmr.2016.10.001

Mars, M., Bronstein, J., & Lusch, R. (2014). Organizations as ecosystems: Probing the value of a metaphor, *University of Toronto Rotman Magazine*, Winter, 72-77. doi.org/10.1016/j.orgdyn.2012.08.002

McGuinness, T., & Morgan, R. E. (2005). The effect of market and learning orientation on strategy dynamics: The contributing effect of organisational change capability. *European Journal of Marketing*, *39*(11/12), 1306-1326. doi:10.1108/03090560510623271

Meyer, A. D. (1982). Adapting to environmental jolts. *Administrative Science Quarterly*, *27*, 515-537. doi:10.2307/2392528

Morgan, G. (2006). *Images of organization.* Thousand Oaks, CA: Sage.

Oxtoby, B., McGuinness, T., & Morgan, R. (2002). Developing organisational change capability. *European Management Journal, 20*(3), 310-320. doi:10.1016/S0263-2373(02)00047-6

Phelan, L., Henderson-Sellers, A., & Taplin, R. (2013). The political economy of addressing the climate crisis in the Earth system: undermining perverse resilience. *New Political Economy, 18*(2), 198- 226. doi.org/10.1080/13563467.2012.678820

Rafferty, A. E., Jimmieson, N. L., & Armenakis, A. A. (2013). Change readiness: A multilevel review. *Journal of Management, 39*(1), 110-135. doi:10.1177/0149206312457417

Rogers, E. M. (2003). *Diffusion of innovations.* New York, NY: Free Press.

Scaccia, J. P., Cook, B. S., Lamont, A., Wandersman, A., Castellow, J., Katz, J., & Beidas, R. S. (2015). A practical implementation science heuristic for organizational readiness: R= MC2. *Journal of Community Psychology*, *43*(4), 484-501. doi.org/10.1002/jcop.21698

Seville, E., Brunsdon, D., Dantas, A., Le Masurier, J., Wilkinson, S., & Vargo, J. (2006). *Building organisational resilience: A New Zealand approach.* Resilient Organizations Research Programme. Retrieved on December 12, 2013 from the Resilient Organisations website: www.resorgs.org.nz

Somers, S. (2009). Measuring resilience potential: An adaptive strategy for organizational crisis planning. *Journal of Contingencies and Crisis Management, 17*(1), 12-23. doi:10.1111/j.1468-5973.2009.00558.x

Sonnet, M. T. (2016). *Employee behaviors, beliefs, and collective resilience: An exploratory study in organizational resilience capacity* (Doctoral dissertation). Retrieved from ProQuest Dissertations & Theses Global. (Order No. 10063554).

Stephenson, A., Vargo, J., & Seville, E. (2010). Measuring and comparing organisational resilience in Auckland. *Australian Journal of Emergency Management, The, 25*(2), 27.

Sutcliffe, K. M. (2005). Information handling challenges in complex systems. *International Public Management Journal, 8*(3), 417-424. doi:10.1080/10967490500439875

Teece, D. J., Pisano, G., & Shuen, A. (1997). Dynamic capabilities and strategic management. *Strategic Management Journal, 18*(7), 509-533.

Tillement, S., Cholez, C., & Reverdy, T. (2009). Assessing organizational resilience: An interactionist approach. *M@n@gement, 12*(4), 230-264.

Van Der Vegt, G. S., Essens, P., Wahlström, M., & George, G. (2015). Managing risk and resilience. *Academy of Management Journal, 58*(4), 971-980. doi.org/10.5465/amj.2015.4004

Vogus, T. J., & Sutcliffe, K. M. (2007, October). Organizational resilience: Towards a theory and research agenda. In *Systems, man and cybernetics, 2007. ISIC. IEEE International Conference*

Weick, K. E. (1988). Enacted sensemaking in crisis situations. *Journal of Management Studies*, *25*(4), 305-317.

Weick, K. E. (1990). The vulnerable system: An analysis of the Tenerife air disaster. *Journal of Management*, *16*(3), 571-593.

Weick, K. E. (1993). The collapse of sensemaking in organizations: The Mann Gulch disaster. *Administrative Science Quarterly*, *38*, 628-652. doi:10.2307/2393339

Weick, K. E. (2010). Reflections on enacted sensemaking in the Bhopal disaster. *Journal of Management Studies*, *47*(3), 537-550. doi:10.1111/j.1467-6486.2010.00900.x

Weick, K. E., & Sutcliffe, K. M. (2011). *Managing the unexpected: Resilient performance in an age of uncertainty* (Vol. 8). San Francisco, CA: John Wiley & Sons.

Weick, K. E., Sutcliffe, K. M., & Obstfeld, D. (2005). Organizing and the process of sensemaking. *Organization Science*, *16*(4), 409-421. doi: 10.1287/orsc.1050.0133

Weick, K. E., Sutcliffe, K. M., & Obstfeld, D. (2008). Organizing for high reliability: Processes of collective mindfulness. *Crisis Management*, *3*(1), 81-123.

Woods, D. D. (2015). Four concepts for resilience and the implications for the future of resilience engineering. *Reliability Engineering & System Safety*, *141*, 5-9. doi.org/10.1016/j.ress.2015.03.018

About the Author

Marie Sonnet, PhD became interested in the people side of change during her years of work in applying process improvement science to business initiatives in a variety of industries. She noted that it was not effective to simply add readiness to a project plan. More could be done proactively to create a ready collective capacity in the organization for a resilient response to planned and unplanned change. She saw an unrecognized and underutilized asset and needed to know which characteristics to observe and develop. As a practitioner scholar, she continues her research and practice in this area, particularly as a Fielding Graduate University Institute for Social Innovation Fellow. Dr. Sonnet lives in Pittsburgh, PA and may be reached at msonnet@ email.fielding.edu or by visiting her website at www.mariesonnet.com.

CHAPTER 5

ECOTONES: HOW INTERSECTIONAL DIFFERENCES SPUR ADAPTATION AND RESILIENCE

Pearl L. Seidman, PhD
Brookings Legis Congressional Fellow
Fielding Graduate University Alumna

Abstract

At its essence, resilience is an adaptive response to change. It is well documented that change is most evident in transition zones where disparate communities intersect. Known as an ecotone, this meeting place of differences is typically characterized by greater diversity, tension, adaptation, and resilience. A phenomenon derived from ecology, this study lies at the intersection of natural and social sciences. Group interviews with Korean American cultural connectors in Howard County, Maryland and their counterparts from other cultures provided a descriptive window into a clearly identifiable cultural ecotone. In this environment, tension was provoked within community as well as from cross community differences. Diversity expanded reservoirs of options. Cultural connectors created new resources, services, and community corridors fueled by their drive, agency, and ability to navigate systems. This cultural ecotone provoked adaptation and suggest it as a sensitive place to monitor resilience in the face of disturbance. Findings provided synaptic insights across, too often, disparate sciences.

Keywords: ecotones, cultural ecotones, Korean Americans, edge effects, diversity, tension, adaptive capacity, adaptive potential, resilience, biocultural diversity, group interviews, intersubjective research

Intersections as the Crossroads of Change

The diversity encountered at intersections is a catalyst for change. In ecology, the intersection of distinct communities is known as an ecotone, literally "house of tension." This transition zone typically has greater diversity, a stimulant for tension and building block for adaptive capacity, a critical element of resilience. The cultural ecotone was revealed in the experiences of those who functioned as bridges or "cultural connectors" (Han, 2012) at the confluence of the Korean American and other communities in Howard County, Maryland (Seidman, 2014).

Identified by community leaders, sixteen noted cultural connectors participated in group and individual interviews. They described spanning dynamics and stress fractures, as often within communities as between them. As individuals adapted and increased their personal agency in response to invited and uninvited change, community resources and leadership networks grew. A model is provided to assess progressive stages of individual and community adaptation.

Inarguably part of nature, our claims of commonalities with and distinctions from nature have fluctuated across cultures and over time. Resilience depends on our interdependent life support system. Social-ecological knowledge systems advance and spark when they draw from each other. Understanding the complex systems that contribute to individual and community resilience requires cross-disciplinary exchange. This relational research explored disciplinary linkage and applicability.

Ecological and Cultural Ecotones

The ecological ecotone is a transition or intermediary zone between two or more distinct adjacent communities containing organisms from each community as well as species living only in the ecotone

(Odum, 1971). These dynamic junctures have a profound influence on the adjacent ecosystems (Hou & Walz, 2016). Ecotones can be gradual or abrupt; naturally occurring (marine and terrestrial) or anthropologically impacted (urban-farmland-wildland). Shorelines are archetypal, but other spatial examples include the interface of tundra and forest, mangroves and coral reefs, savanna and dessert, rocky and sandy beaches, ground surface and air. Ecotones are also temporal transitions—dusk and dawn, wet and dry phases, generational succession, or disturbed and undisturbed patches.

The cultural ecotone is the intersection between distinct cultures where there is interaction and exchange of knowledge, skills, and resources (Turner, Davidson-Hunt, & O'Flaherty, 2003). Throughout history, humans chose ecotones for settlement given increased diversity of food, medicine, and shelter. In earlier civilizations, neutral ports of trade emerged in between autonomous political entities providing safe and neutral exchange. Often biological and cultural ecotones coincided. The long-term viability of a system is "best understood by studying the edge between systems rather than each homogenous system individually" (Gallaway, 2005, p. 708). Cultural ecotones are referenced in archaeology, anthropology, economics, urban planning, sociology, and biocultural literatures.

Frederic Clements coined the word ecotone in 1904 (p. 153) from the Greek, house (*eco*) of tension (*tonos*). The confluence of differences could be beneficial in enhancing function, resources, and services, or inequitable if benefits are not mutually derived. Tension cannot be fully grasped without an appreciation of a world in which diversity and unity, growth and decomposition, cooperation and competition, acquiescence and struggle are dynamic complementary oppositional forces. Tension can precipitate conflict, facilitate coexistence, or both. Often seen as creating disequilibrium, tension also serves to preserve stability as a stimulant for adaptation and resilience.

Ecotones as Connective Tissue between Communities

Ecosystems are communities of organisms and their physical environments that interact in a holistic, integrative, and irreducible system of interdependencies (Li, 2000). Flow between the parts are integral to the whole. The concept of biocultural diversity acknowledges the interplay between biological, cultural, and linguistic diversity (Maffi, 2005; Pretty et al. 2009). Environment, language, and culture are quintessential structural components of human ecotones. The need for cultural connectors has existed since the first division of community. They are representatives of and windows into community. They promote exchange, facilitate translation, mitigate conflict, and in modern times help others navigate unfamiliar institutions, processes, and practices.

For this study, Korean American cultural connectors were of interest based on population size and spatial coherence, relatively recent arrival in the county, and the edge effect or cultural contrasts between heritage and adopted place. First used by Aldo Leopold (1933), *edge effect* refers to the edge at which two or more communities meet with simultaneous access to the resources of differentiated environments such as food or cover. Typically, the greater the structural contrast between two habitats or populations, the greater the edge effect where novelty and change, or resistance to change, are more likely. The nature of these boundaries edges and the flow across offers a bellwether into community well-being.

The United States/Korean Edge Effect

The cultural ecotone is best observed between distinct cultural communities with sharp social, spatial, and temporal contrasts. Contrast is noticed in the number and magnitude of differences. The edge effect is prominent largely for three reasons. First, Korean immigration was severely restricted until passage of the Hart-Celler Immigration and Nationality Act of 1965. Effective in 1968, the United States allowed

20,000 people from every country in the Eastern Hemisphere, with a ceiling of 170,000, and no quotas for immediate family members to include parents of adult U.S. citizens. Second, there has been a dearth of transcultural interaction between Korea and the United States through the centuries largely up until the Korean War.

Third are cultural and language differences. In the U.S., individualism and individual rights dominate. Individuals are responsible for themselves and their families. Honorifics are used in titles prior to a name in formal settings, for some occupations, and in the military; otherwise they are infrequent. The limited use of honorifics conveys the ideals of egalitarian culture. For Koreans, group integration and tightly knit familial and affinity groups are valued. Strength is based on cohesion. Korean language is highly honorific; verb conjugations and noun inflections serve to maintain hierarchy and transmit culture. Vocabulary and word endings vary by age, status, and relationship (Yoon, 2004). Belonging is valued over uniqueness. Contrasts and commonalties are portrayed in findings from participant vantage points.

Korean Americans in Howard County

Howard County, the area of study, is part of a region from northern Baltimore to northern Virginia that is home to the third largest population of Korean Americans in the United States (Table 1).

The first Koreans settled in Howard County in the early 1970s. Fueled largely by good schools and Korean information bureaus, migration has been dramatic and sustained in Howard County since the early 1970s. Currently those of Korean heritage are largely first through second generation with grandchildren marking the third generation of the earliest arrivals (Table 2).

Table 1

*Major Metropolitan Areas for Korean American Residence
within the United States*

Order	Metropolitan Statistical Areas	Number
1	Los Angeles-Long Beach-Anaheim, CA	310,861
2	New York-Newark-Jersey City, NY-NJ-PA	204,642
3	Washington-Arlington-Alexandria, DC-VA-MD-WV	80,541
4	Chicago-Naperville-Elgin, IL-IN-WI	55,595
5	Seattle-Tacoma-Bellevue, WA	52,267
6	Atlanta-Sandy Springs-Roswell, GA	44,753
7	San Francisco-Oakland-Hayward, CA	43,362
8	Philadelphia-Camden-Wilmington, PA-NJ-DE-MD	34,591
9	Dallas-Ft. Worth-Arlington, TX	32,146
10	San Jose-Sunnyvale-Santa Clara, CA	28,731
11	Riverside-San Bernardino-Ontario, CA	26,736
12	Baltimore-Columbia-Towson, MD	24,348

Note. From U.S. Census Bureau (2015).

Table 2

Growth in Howard County of Korean Heritage Population

Year	1980	1990	2000	2010
Total Population	118,572	187,328	247,842	287,085
Korean Population	625	2,369	6,188	12,333
Percentage of County Population	0.5%	1.3%	2.5%	4.3%
Percentage Korean Decennial Growth		279.0%	161.2%	99.3%

Note. From Maryland State Data Center (2011).

Asian relocation to Howard County dramatically exceeds that of both the United States and Maryland (Table 3) with Koreans representing the second largest number of foreign born from Asia (Figure 1).

Table 3

Foreign-Born Birth Region Comparisons for U.S., Maryland, and Howard County

	Foreign-Born Population	Asia	Latin America	Africa	Europe
United States	13.2%	30.1%	51.5%	4.6%	11.3%
Maryland	14.7%	33.0%	39.5%	16.3%	9.9%
Howard County	19.9%	70.6%	17.6%	12.4%	8.0%

Note. From U.S. Census Bureau (2016).

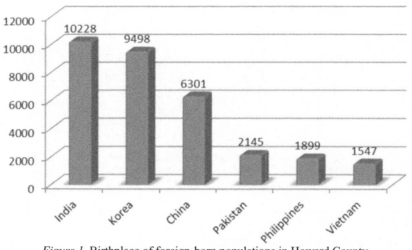

Figure 1. Birthplace of foreign-born populations in Howard County
(U.S. Census Bureau, 2016).

Howard County's eastern suburbs are proximate to north-south interstate corridors between Baltimore and Washington, DC. The juxtaposition of this suburban corridor between two distinctly different urban cities, is itself an ecotone. This contiguous interface provides access to federal, state, corporate, commercial, agricultural, and entrepreneurial sources of employment. Howard County's Asian population is largely clustered along this more populated suburban corridor as are many other ethnic and racial communities in a biocultural ecotone that sustains diversity.

Quality education was a driving factor in relocation for Asian Americans especially attracted to schools with high Scholastic Aptitude Test scores. The cultural investment in education is noted in educational attainment. Maryland is fourth nationally at 38.4% of those age 25 and older holding a bachelor's degree or higher. Korean attainment in Howard County is 54.9% (U.S. Census Bureau, 2015).

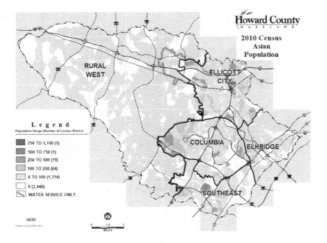

Figure 2. Residential distribution of Howard County's Asian population, 2010 Census
(with permission of the Howard County, MD Department
of Planning and Zoning, 2013).

Migration and Adaptive Capacity

Migration disrupts what was previously normative through physical and psychological relocation inviting shape shifting of identity, culture, language, livelihood, and relationships. The certainty and stability of what was customary is unsettled with even foundational premises subject to question. Adaptation is tested. Adaptive capacity is a dynamic ability of an individual, community, or system based on inherent abilities and those built in anticipation of or in response to external circumstances over time. At the community level, adaptive capacity is the community's ability to access resources and agile infrastructure for reconfiguration in response to uncertainty and change (Norris, Stevens, Pfefferbaum, Wyche, & Pfefferbaum, 2008). At all levels, adaptive capacity includes the ability to operate within boundary ranges in the face of change or to extend the range of environments at which adaptation occurs (Gallopin, 2006).

Disturbance, like migration, may cause vulnerability or expose it. Given sufficient capacity, resilience may require reduction of needs or expansion over a range of options (e.g., use of available material and resources, altered processes, or invention). Adaptive processes are not sufficiently understood in either social or ecological sciences, adding impetus for this study.

Resilience

Adaptation relies on intrinsic and learned abilities and processes. Resilience is an adaptive response. The relationship between tension, adaptability, and resilience is shown in Figure 3.

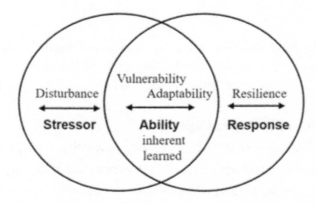

Figure 3. Relationships: stressors, vulnerability, adaptability, and resilience. Adapted from Engle (2011).

Resilient systems maintain themselves in the face of disturbance. In a seminal paper, C. S. Holling (1973) argued that resilience *is not* about the amplitude and frequency of oscillations that measure deviations and return to a static equilibrium state—essentially the rate of recovery or what he referred to as engineering resilience. Rather, Holling recognizes the possibility of multiple equilibria in what he terms ecological resilience. Movement between multiple states sustains internal structures in the face of unpredictability and complexity. He defined resilience more broadly as the ability of a system with mutually reinforcing processes and structures to withstand disruption without collapsing into a fundamentally altered state or new order. Holling conceptualized resilience as maintaining existence; recognizing stability and instability as structural existential tensions. Persistence is characterized by variability not constancy; flexibility rather than rigidity. Constancy may signal system vulnerability, rather than equilibrium.

Rapid detection and response are important, as are the quality and connectedness of relationships in a system. Reactions depend on the response pool available. "The more homogeneous the environment in space and time, the more likely is the system to have low fluctuations and low resilience" (Holling, 1973, p. 18). Instability in the face of the unknown requires a divergent reserve of responses to absorb, buffer, and change. Ability to self-organize, learn, and adapt are key (Resilience Alliance, 2018).

Community resilience became a focus of cross-disciplinary literature in the 1990s. Norris et al. (2008) surveyed ecological and social sciences definitions of community resilience. They defined resilience as, "a process linking a set of networked adaptive capacities to a positive trajectory of functioning and adaptation in constituent populations after a disturbance" (p. 131). Common social-ecological themes included functional diversity, cross-scale interaction (e.g., local, state, national across time), rapid access to social and natural capital, ability to plan and act spontaneously across loosely coupled but cooperative systems, and incremental and transformational learning to further build capacity (Gunderson, 2009). The definition used by Norris et al. addressed strategies for disaster readiness. This resilience definition is used for its social-ecological consilience. It embraces systems and community in alignment with Hollings' ecological resilience—withstanding disturbance without community collapse or reformation into a fundamentally altered state.

The cultural connectors working in the transition zone between distinct communities provide a unique lens into interactivity between diversity, tension, adaptive capacity, and resilience. These cultural bridges also provide insight into the interdependence between individual and community resilience where neither can be understood in isolation.

Relational Research Method

Relational research methods (Bradbury & Lichtenstein, 2000) highlight interdependent and intersubjective construction of meaning. Beyond the mechanics of data collection, analysis, and reporting, relational research is cognizant of the intrinsic relationships, interactions, and dynamics that take place and the field on which they unfold. This research orientation underscores both ways of knowing and being as a researcher. Relational inquiry requires a stance of humility. "Humility means yielding and honoring other possible ways of knowing" and "not knowing thus, giving way to streams of certainty, for waves of ambiguity" (SooHoo, 2013, p. 201).

Four participant dyads for each of two primary group interviews were composed of a Korean American cultural connector living in Howard County and a functional counterpart from another cultural community. Potential participants were approached based on published records and local networks within the Korean community. Sources included non-profit organizations, civic/political associations, church leadership, schools, and business. Participant group members also provided recommendations.

Pre-selection interviews ensured participants were functional cultural connectors. Selectees then nominated a cross-cultural counterpart with whom they worked for goal accomplishment, also pre-screened prior to inclusion. Collectively participants represented local, state, federal and non-profit spheres. Of 16 participants, 9 were of Korean heritage, all foreign-born arriving in the U.S. from early childhood to their late 20s. Seven others were of African, Asian, and European descents. This categorization belies the rich cultural intersectionality of participant experiences. As one participant humorously recounted, he was "made in China, packaged in Taiwan, and delivered to America" (Li, personal interview, January 29, 2018).

Individual and group interviews beyond pre-screening were recorded with permission. Questions were semi-structured. Participants also added their questions in the moment. The process became one of co-inquiry and joint discovery. Acknowledged by participants, new introductions, information, and perspectives accrued. The group setting was consonant with the collective nature of Korean and other Confucian-based cultures in which relationships order societal structure. Group interviews reinforced connectedness and revealed the process of thinking together to expose variant perspectives. Beyond words, insight came from the interplay of language skills and social hierarchies influenced by culture, age, generation, gender, status, and perceived success.

Thematic analysis was used to synthesize data. A report provided to participants elicited responses from 13 of 16. A central consideration was honoring participant voices through accurate portrayal. Respondents confirmed, suggested corrections, clarified content, and provided additional insights. Follow-up and interpretive verification strengthened face and content validity. All participant quotes are attributed with permission.

The Korean American and "Other" Ecotone in Action Diversity

Learning is integral to adaptation. The edge effect pushes its extent. South Korea is widely noted as being one of the most uniform nations in the world with one language and only a few small ethnic minorities. Although the United States has one official language, it has many heritage languages as a result of being a magnet for resettlement from across the globe. In Howard County, one in five residents are foreign born (U.S. Census Bureau, 2016). Howard County students represent 148 countries with 117 languages (Howard County Public

School System, 2018). Cross-cultural understanding was particularly challenging for the first generation-Koreans that came to Howard County when the county had few Korean or Asian residents.

> Forty years ago, Korea used to be one of the most homogeneous cultures. We were people that did not accept any other culture. I grew up in a culture where ... you don't have an opinion. Don't think, don't do anything out of the norm, which means don't be creative... That was something that I thought I should go ahead and accept. I didn't know any other way in those days. I'm in a society that I don't have to do that. That kind of free thinking really helped me. I can be myself and I'm okay about speaking out... People who knew me all along said I am transformed. What that means is that I was really obedient, softly spoken, do as told as women. Somehow, I'm very free, creative, outspoken... So, they think that I am very strange now. (S. Song, personal interview, April 1, 2013)

Because of the novelty, encounter ignited options for action. The ecotone made overt and subtle cultural boundaries evident. Script and counterscript provide a third space which is "polycontextual, multivoiced, and multiscripted" (Gutiérrez, Baquedan-López, & Tejeda, 1999, p. 287). Individual and environment informed the range of possible variations. The ability to access a greater cultural repertoire contributed to individual and community adaptive capacity.

Intersectional Identity

Identity proved to be a central part of the cultural ecotone. Heritages of the inclusive "Other" in this research included African American, Hispanic, Chinese, Taiwanese, and European. While naming conventions like Korean American, Chinese American, or African American evoke past and present, they may not authentically capture either identity or belonging.

Although most individuals of Korean descent identified themselves as Korean American, one individual proudly referred to himself as American Korean. In 1970, Mr. Kim arrived in Howard County with his wife as one of the first four Korean families moving to a predominately White, largely segregated area (91.4% White; 8.1% Negro; 0.5% all other races[1] Bureau of the Census, 1973). Mr. Kim's identity, values, and sense of belonging were transformed.

> My identity is American Korean... When I first came
> to the U.S., I considered myself Korean American,
> 80% Korean/20% American, because my identity was
> too strong in being Korean. However, today I con-
> sider [myself] 80% American/20% Korean. Recently
> when I visited South Korea, my appearance looks
> Korean, however, I am American in the inside,   and
> people can recognize this when I speak to them. (S.
> U. Kim, personal communication, February 20, 2012)

In spite of the ascriptions of others based on appearance and accent, or because of it, Mr. Kim's identity was deeply held. Growth in Howard County went from 4 Korean households in 1970 to 4,143 in 2015 bringing pronounced change (U.S. Census Bureau, 2015).

The county's rural, social, political, and economic terrain pivoted with the development of the planned community, Columbia, in 1967. Revolutionary urban planning for its time, its founding values were racial and economic integration, openness and inclusion, and growth of people in community. A new town inspired new leaders. One participant was the first Black Howard County Council member elected in 1982. He spoke about the hate-filled racial slurs that assaulted him during his run for election more than three decades ago (V. Gray, personal interview, September 9, 2011). He prevailed in part due to the movement of educated, ethnically and racially diverse populations at the crossroads of change.

Cultural connectors embraced their "otherness" in the context of dominant culture, while those in the dominant culture spoke of sensitization to their White privilege. Experiences with discrimination and privilege proved to be compelling reasons for at least two participants who entered local government service. "When you're born White in Howard County, you're born with a certain amount of privilege automatically, and you need to go out and help people who maybe don't know the ropes or don't have the contacts that you have and advocate for them" (C. Watson, personal interview, September 9, 2011).

Identity emerges through and is polished by intersectional rubbing against differences. The polishing rocks are themselves complex in composition, e.g., environment, history, heritage, lineage, culture, language, class, physical attributes, gender, generation, education, occupation, life experience, achievement, and roles. Identity emerges, but it and its expression are not fixed. Self-identification is a difficult and situationally dependent question defined at a point and place in time.

> How do I identify myself? That's a tough question, depends on where you are, who you're surrounded by. Like if I was in Korea, I would feel very American. If I'm in America, I feel more Korean. If I'm in a room full of people that are all American, I feel very Korean. If I thought about it I would say, "that's an unfair question, let me explain" and it would be a long dialogue. (C. Sung, personal interview, September 9, 2011)

Marrying a cultural other provides close encounter with difference. In collective Asian cultures, the use of words like me and mine are relatively rare in favor of adjectives like us and ours. Ordering food illustrates how American individualistic and Korean collectivistic cultural and linguistic norms order worlds.

My husband orders what he likes first. He thinks,
"my food, my portion." For me, my children go first
and I order last. I order different food. If they order
something and don't like it, I will eat it. In our culture
we share food. We always have separate soup and
rice bowls. Everything else we share, whoever we
are with—good things and bad things. If one of us is
sick, your sickness is my sickness. I am us. Koreans
say "our children," not "my children," because all our
families belong together. We all belong to each other.
(MiSchill Kim, personal interview, April 1, 2014)

Eating together informs connectedness like few other rituals.

Polarities—Individuality and Connectedness

Of particular note was the presence of integrative thinking, the ability to
see dualities (opposite attributes that function together) associated with
creativity (Maslow, 1968). Distinctive identities were strongly held as
was connectedness. Diversity was a source of pride and an opportunity
to transcend differences by integrating rather than assimilating.
Assimilation is "leave my culture behind, take the majorities," while
integration is "keep my culture, take from both; keep both" (R. Pope,
personal interview, September 9, 2011). Cultural identity was important
to maintain while concurrently seeking social acceptance and equitable
access to resources and opportunity. Acquisition of new behavioral,
cognitive, and somatic traits involves hybridization—being of both
cultures while not being fully of either—integration and differentiation;
location and dislocation; belonging and otherness.

Human interconnectedness was articulated by many. Individual
identity mattered a great deal without contradiction between uniqueness
and wholeness. A striking commonality was the international
experiences of many that typified the reach of cultural exposure. Many
individuals worked or traveled extensively overseas or worked with

foreign-born populations from a mosaic of heritages. Their experiences routinely brought them to the multicultural commons. One person identified himself by his Korean heritage, but most importantly as part of a unified whole. Bridges were unnecessary between cultures as they were already connected. Others saw themselves and their work as functional bridges. Worldview and self-identity were stamped by spatial realities and psychological/spiritual dimensions.

Generally, the tone across interviews respected individuality while working for the collective good valuing uniqueness and connectedness, not one or the other. Dualities, paradoxes, or other dynamic tensions brought up included tradition and novelty, idealism and pragmatism, inclusion and exclusion, collaboration and competition, cost and benefit, harmony and conflict, collectivism and individualism.

Endogenous Barriers – Tension Within

Endogenous and exogenous sources of tension were both expressed by foreign-born participants. While external tension was anticipated, three sources of internalized community tension also surfaced: generational experiences, cultural transmission and persistence, and internal focus as a limiting factor in impact of cultural connectors. All three themes poignantly exemplify stressors within the temporal ecotone—the transition zone between stages of immigrant evolution, generations, and succession.

The Asian American participants were all either first or what has been described as *1.5 generation*. First generation, *ilse*, applies to those foreign-born arriving in the US as late teenagers or older; 1.5 generation, *ilchŏm ose*, refers to those arriving before or during adolescence with increased plasticity of bicultural and bilingual skills; second generation, *ise*, applies to those born in the US. The term 1.5 generation was initially coined by sociologist Rubén Rumbaut (1988). The "arrival by" definition varies from ages 13 to 17 or pre-adult varies across studies. The decimal signifies the experience of being neither here nor there, neither wholly one generation nor the other. In the early 1980s, K.W. Lee used the term "twilight" as a generational descriptive (Park, 1999), an explicit reference to the temporal ecotone.

The 1.5 generation find themselves in between expectations of their parents and their own and between country of origin and current place, with tugs in both directions. They act as intermediaries. Parents are the authorities, but children may be translators and navigators. Quotes from first and 1.5-generation males respectively are illustrative.

> Eighty percent of Koreans come here for their children's education. They work long hours in grocery, liquor, or cleaning businesses. The 1.5 generation is left at home for long hours. There is a culture problem within the Korean community. Every 10 years there is a different culture that I have to deal with in the family and at church. One-third of marriages now are mixed marriages. (S. U. Kim, personal interview, September 9, 2011)

> At one time I was involved with 19 committees. The community expects it from those that work in professional fields. There are both pull and push factors. The pull is from driven, type "A" personalities who wish to extend their professional capacities and involvement. The push factor is from the 1.0 generation, also known as a frozen culture. They depend and expect to live vicariously through their children. (J. Ahn, personal interview, June 10, 2011)

It is a liminal space for both first and 1.5 generations involving displacement, uncertain strategies for navigating place, role reversal, and sacrifice. Purposefulness in providing children with a better life explicitly or implicitly instills a sense of debt. Children are caught between their own aspirations and those of their parents. Traditional roles are upended and collective identity creates tension in an individualistic society.

Parents want to preserve culture through affiliation with ethnic churches and after school and weekend activities. Children want belonging with peer groups. The social pressures to fit into both cultures are increased. So are the consequences of fitting into neither. Fitting too well has resulted in the code term "Banana" or "Twinkie" (yellow on the outside; white on the inside) used by the foreign born to describe the second generation and by the second generation self-descriptively.

Persistence and Change

Some contributing sources of Korean community insularity were noted. "Korea has historically been known as the 'Hermit Kingdom.' We're used to staying amongst ourselves and saying we can survive by ourselves, we can make this work without other people's help" (C. Sung, personal interview, September 9, 2011). The need to protect Korean cultural identity is rooted in many outsider national and cultural usurpation attempts. In 1905, the Korean peninsula became a Japanese protectorate until its full annexation by Japan from 1910-1945. Japan confiscated and burned books on geography, culture, and history. Korean names, language, and religion were prohibited in attempts to obliterate culture; monetary and financial systems were reorganized; land and crops were appropriated.

Geography and history increased determination to retain heritage through family and institutional transmission for the county's recent generations.

> We want to make sure that their Korean heritage and
> culture's preserved somehow; that they know what
> Chuseok is, [Korean Thanksgiving]; that they know
> how to speak the Korean language; that they are
> familiar with Korean food.... Here at most its third

186

generation and here even a third-generation Korean
American understands Korean at least. They might
not be able to speak it, but they'll understand it. (C.
Sung, personal interview, September 9, 2011)

A Pew Research poll (2013) indicated that Korean Americans, more
than any other U.S. Asian group, want to retain their native language
(62%) and connect with friends that are of the same heritage (58%).
Heritage communities provide a tangible sense of belonging. Cultural
preservation is critical in maintaining identity, collective values, and
social cohesion within the context of a diverse society. The cultural
ecotone is disquieting with multiple stressors, including issues of fit,
competing values, and a new status quo with the erosion or replacement
of the old one. Community creates a buffer area to mitigate the tension
and risks associated with being a minority. The church is the heart of
community for many families and individuals shaping the immigrant
experience. Nationally, 71% of Korean Americans are Christian
compared to 29% of South Korea's population (Pew Research Center,
2014).

Churches serve as sanctuary for faith, culture, social interaction,
learning, and support. Churches unite people in observance of traditions
and celebration of Korean holidays. They build provide status through
positions as lay leaders, deacons, and elders. Members support each
other through sharing contacts, resources, or "how to" instructions. For
the first generation, churches provide a place for common language
and culture; a gathering place with other foreign born. For the second-
generation English ministries support bi-cultural practices balancing
change with continuity. Even in English ministries, local Korean
churches tend to be homogeneous.

Community self-reliance exacts a cost. While church- and
community-based after-school and weekend activities transmit
language, values, and standards, they distance the next generation from

their peers. Cultural retention becomes an increasingly intentional maintenance function in pluralistic ecologies. While group cohesion is valued, the calibration of cross-community interactions was considered not to be well-tuned by cultural connectors.

A unified voice within the Korean American or larger Asian community was seen as politically necessary. "There are divergent views and different agendas which present another layer of obstacles in providing a clear voice. We are pushing to the same goal in different ways. Later generations will improve, but there will always be some boundaries" (B. Chang, personal interview, March 17, 2013). Needs for respect are hierarchically defined. Autocratic rules conflict with democratic decision making. For example, others may take credit for accomplishments given higher position or elder status (MiSchill Kim, personal interview, April 5, 2013). The availability of skilled leaders was a prominent theme:

> We learn to be leaders. I've seen more division than unification among the first-generation Korean immi-grants; however, fortunately their 1.5- and second-generation children seem to be doing better. As long as they care for one another, first-generation Koreans are giving to each other, but as soon as their feelings are hurt [Koreans call it hurting hearts, which in their minds is much deeper than hurt feelings], they cut off the relationship right away and it becomes very dif-ficult for them to forgive each other and equally hard to bring the relationship back to where it once was.
> (A. Kwon, personal interview, March 17, 2013)

Time and energy are often channeled into family and community. For first generations, being a sole proprietor typically means that work, taking care of children, and perhaps attending church when/ if the business is closed becomes all consuming. For 1.5 and second generations, commitments are marshaled to meet the needs of parents and new immigrants. Communal cultural values underscore this pressure. This self-reinforcing loop restricts the ascendance of cross-cultural leaders.

> There is an expression in the Korean culture called frozen culture. The age that you immigrate is the culture that you maintain. I came in 1974. The songs and the drama and the culture that I have, the manners and the traditions, are 1970s... I have not lived up to the current trends, so to speak. The churches also have the same kind of frozen culture and they have a hard time breaking out of that mold. Our church is trying to do that with [a] 1.5-generation pastor, who is bilingual, bicultural, and is the first time that our church, in thirty years of history, had a pastor who could interact with community at large without having a translator next to him. And it is a wonderful liberation, having freedom that we enjoy, I enjoy, because I had to accommodate many of those translation moments. (J. Ahn, personal interview, September 9, 2011)

The crossroads of ministries and generations; tradition and change can be both precarious and unifying.

Exogenous Barriers to Belonging

Appearance-based assumptions about nationality call into question American identity. "Physical features cause boundaries even when we are more Americanized" (MiSchill Kim, personal interview, March 17, 2013). "Back home you were the dominant culture. Here you are the minority and on the fringe of society where people ask you where are you from? You are not the dominant culture or even the second dominant culture. There is conflict among minority cultures" (Min Kim, personal interview, March 17, 2013). "Where are you from?" turns corrosive when it becomes a question of complexion and when the intended or unintended premise is "you must not be from this country."

Conflict among minorities is exacerbated by the myth of the "model minority" cited as a prevalent Pan-Asian caricature. Minority creates "Othering"; model identifies one's place in the hierarchy of other minorities. Inferred is that intelligence, attainment orientation, and predisposition for science, technology, and math are culturally determined. The expression simultaneously contracts and expands social distance—we approve of you, but you're not one of us. Categorization sculpts with coarse tools creating boundaries between "us" and "you" and "those others." A Pan-Asian blender effect ensures that national and individual differences become obscured through partial or distorted representation. False expectations mask needs preventing them from being met, provide pressure to excel associated with psychological distress, create interracial tensions, and conceal the fact that discrimination is occurring (Choi, Godina, & Ro, 2013; Yi & Museus, 2016).

Foreign-born communities are immersed in American culture through school, business, and professional interactions. For the dominant culture, cultural learning is optional. "They are in their own comfort zones. It's really hard for them to open the door, so it's really difficult for me to connect with them" (S. Song, personal interview, April 1, 2013). The insulation of the dominant culture is frequently invisible. Comfort zones act as social barriers thick with distance, salient with consequence. Absent cultural inquiry, communication is stifled and the benefit of alternate perspectives is lost in the certainty of one's own views.

Of concern, too, was the disproportionately smaller voice of the Asian community when compared by size to other minority groups. With strong Asian values on education, no Chinese or Koreans had served on Howard County's Board of Education (Li, personal interview, March 17, 2013). The absence of Asian involvement was attributed to bias and Confucian culture, which values people not speaking up. Political involvement is more than nascent. Evidence is provided by the participation of three current and former elected officials in this research. In early 2014, the Republican gubernatorial candidate held the first fundraiser of his campaign with the Korean American community in Howard County (Lazarick, 2014). A second-generation Chinese American public health physician became a Maryland state delegate in 2015 and is running for the state senate in 2018.

Cultural Adaptive Capacity

Adaptation of person to environment is text and subtext throughout all findings—identity and community development; needs, options for action, and individual/institutional response sets; relationships across generations and with cultural "others"; and growth of social capital. A heuristic developed by Young-chan Han, an educator and research participant, is most useful in understanding cultural adaptive potential. The model in Figure 4 echoes Ms. Han's immigrant experiences and her extensive work with foreign-born populations in Howard County and statewide through the Maryland State Department of Education. These stages of development are scalable from individuals to communities.

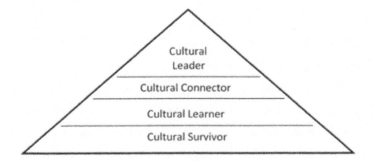

Figure 4. Stages of immigrant parent involvement in schools (Han, 2012).

These stages describe the ability to acquire culture, language, and resources within and across communities. An individual or community can be at one stage for some domains and in different stages for others. Survivors are dependent on others to act as interpreters and navigators. Access can be limited for full immersion single proprietor businesses or for those with interactions limited to fellow survivors. Churches, schools, non-profits, and county services facilitate learning. Learning stimulates movement from dependence to independence to interdependence. Cultural connectors enable civic engagement. Community leaders build relationships, strengthen network capacity, and institutionalize exchange mechanisms through intercultural social and work groups, associations, boards, and committees.

Advancement signifies progress from dislocation to location to co-construction. An individual could be satisfied as a cultural survivor or learner in a context that is safe and comfortable. Velocity of transition depends on capacity, determination, personal agency, and access. However, a community is vulnerable when disturbance occurs without sufficient pathways to tap into trusted resources.

Adaptation and Resilience in Action

Given the definition used, community resilience as the positive functioning and adaptation after a disaster, could only be inferred. There was a weather disturbance during the study which will be subsequently discussed, but while of some magnitude, it did not threaten the community foundation.

While referred to as connectors, participants proved to be deft cultural leaders. Their cultural pliability and intercultural ability contributed innovations in larger proportions than their numbers suggest. Impact extended to education, healthcare, eldercare, crisis mitigation and intervention.

Education

Since 2006, foreign-born parents have benefited from an inventive six-week International Parent Leadership Program (IPLP) developed by Young-chan Han. International education practices and parent engagement in schools vary widely, making local navigation difficult. IPLP provides instruction about policy, curriculum, and school culture to grow those serving as volunteer interpreters, active PTA members, or those involved in other ways. Immigrant parents learn, adapt, transmit knowledge, and harness a greater sphere of influence for their children and others. A dozen years later, IPLP continues as a best practice in Howard and other counties, with adoption spreading to other states.

Efforts by Yen Li, a former principal of the Chinese Language School of Columbia (CLSC), exemplified the importance of cultural bridges. A Chinese woman who arrived in the local area with her children. When one of her children became ill, she used "*ba guan*" or cupping, a treatment commonly used for colds. It bruised the child's back. A teacher noticed and alarmed, called the school administrator, child protection services, and the police. Neither mother nor child spoke English. Considering arrest, the police called the CLSC and hours of negotiation finally brought resolution and an educational relationship between the CLSC and the school system. Additionally, persistent advocacy by Dr. Li over two decades resulted in inclusion of Chinese language instruction, originally piloted in high schools, and now part of world language immersion classes in middle and elementary schools (Li, personal interview, January 28, 2018). Mandarin is the most widely spoken language in the world. The world language program builds cross-cultural understanding at young ages, readies students to be part of a more interconnected world, and helps students from dominant cultures interface with their foreign-born peers.

Healthcare

Addressing a void in culturally and linguistically sensitive and affordable medical services for the wider Asian community, Anne Kwon co-founded a clinic in Howard County working with members of the Korean and Chinese communities. The resulting Asian American Healthcare Center (AAHC) is a non-profit clinic operating since 2008. Volunteer physicians and staff provide services to the uninsured and financially disadvantaged with preventive care and referrals. Culturally competent health practitioners are equipped to understand health disparities unique to Asians populations, traditional practices, and decision-making factors concerning health choices.

Eldercare

Sue Song was instrumental in the county's first culturally-specific unit within an established skilled nursing facility. The idea was conceived when she was president of the Korean American Community Association of Howard County. Opened in 2013 with five beds, this specialized unit is uniquely immersive with Korean food and games and visiting Korean clergy. "A couple of years after the wing was opened, they noticed the rate of falls was high. It turned out that many of the residents with dementia were getting out of bed and sleeping on the floor because they slept that way in Korea." (McDaniels, 2017). What began as an experiment now includes 53 beds with a wait list. Homogenization of services like healthcare and eldercare may standardize practices but superimpose dominate culture while sacrificing knowledge and quality of care.

Emergency Preparedness

On August 28, 2011, Hurricane Irene caused flooding and power outages on the East Coast. It was followed on September 7th by Tropical Storm Lee, which was even more severe causing extensive flooding in Ellicott City which triggered FEMA recovery funding. During the hurricane the preceding week, a Korean man died and two family members were hospitalized as a result of carbon monoxide poisoning caused by generator use (Greisman, 2011).

During the group interview on September 9th, the County Council member representing Ellicott City spoke about that tragedy. Information about hurricane preparedness was conveyed prior to Irene's arrival, but she was uncertain whether posting included two Korean daily newspapers. That was a catalytic moment. People started talking to each other, offering suggestions about effective channels to use in rapidly conveying language sensitive information to the community. Suggestions were made that the local government engage church leaders, service providers, school interpreters, volunteers, and other cultural connectors in place. The county's emergency channels could be supplemented with existing cultural community pathways to quickly and accurately transmit information. Trusted information in cultural context increases the probability of adherence. Diverse communities contribute to a more robust response pool and novel approaches.

Cross-scale Influence

Participants were employed at county, state, and federal levels. Their body of work as connectors also created understanding of cross-scale influence to channel appropriate community services.

> The government may think they know what's best for us, but it's worth it when the government hears directly from the local community. We need to have a system in place to protect people from fraud, educate them on what programs will benefit them, and, at the local level, we can take voices of the people to the state and federal levels for more awareness. It only works when local to state to federal governments are connected. (A. Kwon, personal interview, March 17, 2013)

Seeing connections was the first step in leveraging connections. The examples cited demonstrate that the cultural elasticity of connectors flowed to facilitate that of others within their capacity limits.

Discussion

The importance of the corridor function of connectors in advancing cross-stage adaptation in the cultural ecotone is a key finding. Cultural connectors influence the interfaces at which change occurs. Their contributions built trusted relationships, and not only cultural exposure, but understanding. They not only shaped the quality of the space between communities, they also changed the operating systems of the bordering communities. They were additive resources creating community intersufficiency' in identifying gaps and implementing solutions. Their activities touched people where they lived, worked, learned, worshipped, and governed. Local impacts rippled across communities and sometimes county and state lines.

It is argued that real and perceived tension provide the scaffolding of our natural order. By definition, ecotones require insight into the duality and dynamism of tension, as attested by the experience of those connectors in this study. Diversity caused external tension through stereotypes, access hurdles, and misunderstanding across language, culture, and values of disparate communities. Internal tension was in play and more often voiced in vicarious expectations of parents, parent-child role reversals, personal change/cultural retention, offsets in generational values, and time pressures. Without tension there is no reason to adapt or build adaptive potential. Tension was a trigger for individual and collective elasticity—in behavior, ways of seeing, social networks, and innovation.

There is no resilience without adaptive capacity. Adaptive processes drive resiliency outcomes. Han's (2012) developmental stages are relevant especially in the cultural ecotone where equilibrium shifts are more likely. These stages resonate with Holling's (1973) ecological resilience notion of multiple stable states. In response to disturbance one may fallback as a survivor, learn coping strategies, develop connections to learn from and support others, and perhaps eventually lead. Foreign-born connectors were frustrated that their community had not reached its potential. While they themselves were at the apex as leaders, their community lagged behind in social and political capital. Understanding the stages of adaptation of individuals and communities benefits political and community leaders in targeting true needs, even those behind face-saving veils, with culturally-appropriate interventions. Moreover, insight into the ecotonal dynamics would inform strategies in the context of continuous change and prevention/ mitigation resources in the face of potential existential disturbance.

We are bounded by what we understand and what we can imagine. Diverse resources allow us to exceed those bounds. Ecological and social sciences alike note that monocultures and low diversity create brittle adaptive capacity and low resilience. This research suggests that adaptive processes be studied at eco-cultural interfaces across social and natural sciences. While biological diversity is recognized as a critical element in resilience, what is the role of cultural diversity? This inquiry encourages a view of the space between communities as sites of change to study the in-situ interplay between diversity, tension, adaptive capacity, and resilience.

When we fail to see social-ecological system relationships, we privilege parts over the whole. Public health officials and climate scientists alike increasingly see social-ecological integration as the lens for intervention and prevention/mitigation strategies. Complex systems demand an integrated web of knowledge. Biocultural ecotones provide a bridge between disciplines in the same way that cultural connectors bridge community.

End Notes

[1] In 1970, the Census Bureau grouped race and ethnicity as White, Negro, Indian, Japanese, Chinese, Filipino and all other races.

[2] Term attributed to John Sullivan (2006), Professor of Philosophy Emeritus, Elon University.

References

Bradbury, H., & Lichtenstein, B. M. (2000). Relationality in organizational research: Exploring the space between. *Organization Science, 11*(5), 551-564. doi:10.1287/orsc.11.5.551.15203

Bureau of the Census. (1973, February). *1970 census of population.* Retrieved from Census of Population and Housing: http://www2.census.gov/prod2/decennial/documents/1970a_md-01.pdf

Choi, J., Godina, H., & Ro, Y. E. (2013). Korean-American student perceptions on literacy and identity: Perspectives from an ethnographic case study. *Asia Pacific Journal of Education*, 1-14. doi:10.1080/02188791.2013.856285

Clements, F. E. (1904). *The development and structure of vegetation.* Lincoln, NE: Woodruff-Collins Printing.

Engle, N. L. (2011). Adaptive capacity and its assessment. *Global Environmental Change, 21*, 647-656. doi:10.1016/j.gloenvcha.2011.01.019

Gallaway, T. (2005). Life on the edge: A look at ports of trade and other ecotones. *Journal of Economic Issues, 39*(3), 707-726. doi:10.1080/00213624.2005.11506841

Gallopin, G. C. (2006). Linkages between vulnerability, resilience, and adaptive capacity. *Global Environmental Change, 16*, 293-303. doi: 10.1016/j.gloenvcha.2006.02.004

Greisman, D. (2011, September 1). Two improving in Ellicott City carbon monoxide poisoning that left one dead. *The Baltimore*

Sun. Retrieved from http://www.baltimoresun.com/ph-ho-cf-co-poisoning-0901-20110830-story.html

Gunderson, L. (2009, January). *CARRI Research Report 5 - Comparing ecological and human community resilience.* Retrieved from Community & Regional Resilience Initiative: http://www.resilientus.org/wp-content/uploads/2013/03/Final_Gunderson_1-12-09_1231774754.pdf

Gutiérrez, K. D., Baquedano López, P., & Tejeda, C. (1999). Rethinking diversity: Hybridity and hybrid language practices in the third space. *Mind, Culture, and Activity, 6*(4), 286-303. doi:10.1080/10749039909524733

Han, Y. (2012). From survivors to leaders: Stages of immigrant parent involvement in schools. In E. G. Kugler, *Innovative voices in education: Engaging diverse communities* (pp. 171-186). Lanham, MD: Rowman & Littlefield.

Holling, C. S. (1973). Resilience and stability of ecological systems. *Annual Review of Ecology & Systematics, 4*, 111-123. doi:10.1146/annurev.es.04.110173.000245

Hou, W. & Walz, U. (2016). An integrated approach for landscape contrast analysis with particular consideration of small habitats and ecotones. *Nature Conservation, 14,* 25-39. doi:10.3897/natureconservation.14.7010

Howard County, Maryland Department of Planning and Zoning. (2013). *2010 Census profile of selected social, economic and housing characteristics.* Division of Research.

Howard County Public School System. (2018). *International Student and Family Services.* Retrieved from Howard County Public School System: http://www.hcpss.org/languages/english/

Lazarick, L. (2014, February 24). *Off to the races: Decision time for candidates; running mates needed; incumbent senators challenged; Hogan appeals to Korean Americans.* Retrieved from http://marylandreporter.com/2014/02/24/off-to-the-races-decision-time-for-candidates-running-mates-needed-incumbent-senators-challenged-hogan-appeals-to-korean-americans/

Leopold, A. (1933). *Game management.* New York, NY: Charles Scribner's Sons.

Li, B.-L. (2000, August). Why is the holistic approach becoming so important in landscape ecology? *Landscape and Urban Planning, 50*(1–3), 27–41. doi:10.1016/S0169-2046(00)00078-5

Maffi, L. (2005). Linguistic, cultural, and biological diversity. *Annual Review of Anthropology, 34*, 599-617. doi:10.1146/annurev.anthro.34.081804.120437

Maryland State Data Center. (2011, May 25). *Department of Planning.* Retrieved from https://planning.maryland.gov/MSDC/Documents/Census/Cen2010/sf1/sumyprof/comparison/Howa.pdf

Maslow, A. H. (1968). *Toward a psychology of being.* New York, NY: Von Nostrand Reinhold. doi:10.1037/10793-000

McDaniels, A. (2017, November 24). *Columbia nursing home makes elder Koreans feel at home.* Retrieved from http://www.baltimoresun.com/health/bs-hs-korean-nursing-home-20171120-story.html

Norris, F. H., Stevens, S. P., Pfefferbaum, B., Wyche, K. F., & Pfefferbaum, R. L. (2008). Community resilience as a metaphor, theory, set of capacities, and strategy for disaster readiness. *American Journal of Community Psychology, 41*, 127-50. doi:10.1007/s10464-007-9156-6

Odum, E. P. (1971). *Fundamentals of ecology* (3rd ed.). Philadelphia, PA: W. B. Saunders.

Park, K. (1999). I really do feel I'm 1.5: The construction of self and community by young Korean Americans. *Amerasia Journal*, 129-163. doi:10.17953/amer.25.1.07x6826254g3567w

Pew Research Center. (2013, April 4). *The Rise of Asian Americans.* Retrieved from Pew Research Social & Demographic Trends:

http://www.pewsocialtrends.org/2012/06/19/the-rise-of-asian-americans/

Pew Research Center. (2014, August 12). *6 Facts about South Korea's Growing Christian Population.* Retrieved from http://www.pewresearch.org/fact-tank/2014/08/12/6-facts-about-christianity-in-south-korea/

Pretty, J., Adams, B., Berkes, F., De Athayde, S. F., Dudley, N., Hunn, E., . . . Pilgrim, S. (2009). The intersections of biological diversity and cultural diversity: Towards integration. *Conservation and Society, 7*(2), 100-112. doi:10.4103/0972-4923.58642

Resilience Alliance. (2018). Retrieved from Resilience Alliance: https://www.resalliance.org/resilience

Rumbaut, R. G. & Kenji, I. (1988). *The adaptation of Southeast Asian refugee youth. A comparative study.* Final report to the Office of Resettlement, San Diego State University. Retrieved from http://files.eric.ed.gov/fulltext/ED299372.pdf

Seidman, P. L. (2014). *Ecotones, boundaries, and culture: Intersections of Korean American and other communities in Howard County, Maryland* (Doctoral Dissertation). Fielding Graduate University, Santa Barbara, CA.

SooHoo, S. (2013). Humility within culturally responsive methodologies. In M. Berryman, S. SooHoo, & A. Nevin, *Culturally responsive methodologies* (pp. 199-220). Bingley, United Kingdom: Emerald Group. doi: 10.1108/IJRD-08-2013-0014

Sullivan, J. G. (2006). *Homepage John Greenfelder Sullivan.* Retrieved from Elon University: http://facstaff.elon.edu/sullivan/

Turner, N. J., Davidson-Hunt, I. J. & O'Flaherty, M. (2003). Living on the edge: Ecological and cultural edges as sources of diversity for social-ecological resilience. *Human Ecology, 31*(3), 439-461. doi: 10.1023/A:1025023906459

U.S. Census Bureau. (2015). *2011-2015 American Community Survey 5-Year estimates.* Retrieved from American FactFinder: http://

factfinder2.census.gov/faces/nav/jsf/pages/index.xhtml

U.S. Census Bureau. (2016). *2012-2016 American Community Survey 5-Year estimates.* Retrieved from American FactFinder: http://factfinder2.census.gov/faces/nav/jsf/pages/index.xhtml

Yi, V. & Museus, S. D. (2016). Model minority myth. In J. Stone, R. M. Dennis, P. S. Rizova, A. D.Smith & X. Hou, *The Wiley Blackwell Encyclopedia of Race, Ethnicity, and Nationalism.* John Wiley & Sons, Ltd. doi: 10.1002/9781118663202.wberen528

Yoon, K.-J. (2015). Not just words: Korean social models and the use of honorifics. *Intercultural Pragmatics, 1*(2), 189-210. doi: 10.1515/iprg.2004.1.2.189

About the Author

Pearl L. Seidman, PhD is an avid learner and researcher interested in system relationships. She is currently a Brookings Legis Congressional Fellow working on Capitol Hill on a wide range of policy issues, often diving into the unknown. The majority of her career has been as an applied behavioral scientist for the federal government. She holds a Bachelor of Arts in Psychology from the University of Maryland, a Master of Science in Applied Behavioral Science from Johns Hopkins University, and Master of Arts and doctorate in Human and Organizational Systems from Fielding Graduate University. Her work, Vitality at the Edges: Ecotones and Boundaries in Social and Ecological Systems, was published in the World Future Review, Oct-Nov 2009. Pearl lives in Columbia, Maryland with her husband. Dr. Seidman may be contacted at pseidman@email.fielding.edu.

CHAPTER 6

CRUZANDO PUENTES / CROSSING BRIDGES: BUILDING RESILIENCE THROUGH COMMUNITAS

Connie Corley, PhD; David Blake Willis, PhD;
Diyana Dobberteen, MA; and Eliza von Baeyer, MA
School of Leadership Studies, Fielding Graduate University

Abstract

A cross-disciplinary, multi-university research team comprised of faculty and students from Fielding Graduate University, California State University Los Angeles, and representatives of community partner sites created an opportunity for experiential learning. This scholarship and fieldwork, which highlighted the resilience of a Los Angeles community, were supported through Fielding Graduate University's Social Transformation Project. For over three years, the project provided a laboratory for dialogues across cultures, generations, and institutions/ organizations. The research question guiding this case study was: *"How can a community of practice integrate academic and service settings to promote intergenerational and intercultural mentoring?"* The results of this living learning laboratory were something far more than we expected: *a vibrant community of practice.* We discovered that this temporary community had its own life, culminating in building close personal bonds between participants through sharing stories of resilience. Through *communitas,* community resilience was fostered in which seeds of change could be incubated and allowed to flourish.

Keywords: Resilience, community of practice, social transformation, case study, cultural identity, social identity, *communitas,* intergenerational engagement, visual ethnography

Introduction

In this chapter, the process and outcomes of a multi-year initiative we titled *Cruzando Puentes* ("Crossing Bridges") are presented as they unfolded. The seed was planted when Connie Corley envisioned bringing people together from her two academic affiliations with elders in a retirement home in the larger community of Boyle Heights, an area adjacent to downtown Los Angeles that is rich in history and culture. This work led to engaging with another organization that had emerged from Boyle Heights to counteract the impact of gang violence in the 1990s. Stories of resilience are a thread weaving together this intergenerational/intercultural project that evolved over three years and engaged people of diverse backgrounds in a community of practice.

We first describe *Cruzando Puentes* as a community of practice, discussing resilience and its enhancement through storytelling, focusing on the impact of stories of resilience. Connections we catalyzed between participants revealed *communitas* in each of the three project phases. To reflect on the cultures and resilience that we experienced in Boyle Heights and Los Angeles, we also incorporate images of these communities and connections using visual ethnography.

Cruzando Puentes: Crossing Bridges, Engaging Communities

Cruzando Puentes ("Crossing Bridges" in Spanish) was the name given to collaborative research and a learning laboratory that emerged when funding became available to launch a Social Transformation Project through Fielding Graduate University's Institute for Social Innovation in 2015. The first author, Connie Corley, partnered with David Blake Willis and other faculty, students, and alumni from Fielding to engage with faculty and students from California State University Los Angeles (CSULA) and others to form what Etienne Wenger and others have called a *community of practice* (2000) in the Boyle Heights community east of downtown Los Angeles in conjunction with Hollenbeck Palms Retirement Community and Homeboy Industries.

The primary emphasis of *Cruzando Puentes* was to support the resilience of individuals within a community. Wenger has characterized a community of practice as a joint enterprise in which members are mutually engaged and produce a shared repertoire of resources (2000). Unlike some communities of practice in which members have regular processes like standing meetings, *Cruzando Puentes* created specific opportunities for engagement in each of its three phases, which are described further below.

Our *Cruzando Puentes* community of practice incorporated seven design principles from *Cultivating Communities of Practice: A Guide to Managing Knowledge*: 1) design for evolution, 2) open a dialogue between inside and outside perspectives, 3) invite different levels of participation, 4) develop both public and private community spaces, 5) focus on value, 6) combine the familiar with excitement, and 7) create a rhythm for the community (Wenger, McDermott & Snyder, 2002). Attending to what we saw as "how to design for aliveness" was a key in creating and nurturing our community of practice as one that was appropriate to the cultures of Los Angeles, California.

The ethnographic stories that follow of personal survival and resilience, of elders as well as former gang members, merge together with co-inquiry in the spirit of what anthropologists Victor Turner and Edith Turner have called *communitas* (1974, 2012). Essentially this is an unstructured state in which all members of a community are equal, allowing them to share a common experience. In each phase of the project, experiences and interactions in community created *communitas,* transient states of meaningful exchange which occur through formal or informal rituals such as the sharing of meals (Turner, 2008, in Napier, 2016). Consciously welcoming interaction between individuals who might not typically connect was part of the overall process, and through *communitas,* meaningful stories were shared. The stories of resilience presented here reinforced the resilience of our community of practice and the community members. Central to adaptation is the importance of relationships including family and friendships, although in *communitas* even shorter encounters can elicit an adaptive response or affirmation of adaptation to previously adverse conditions in life. As Turner has noted, "*Communitas* can only be properly conveyed through stories" (2012, p. 1).

Enhancing Resilience Through Storytelling in the Context of *Communitas*

Resilience has been examined and defined in a broad range of contexts but here resilience is considered as both an adaptive response to adversity and seen in the context of maintaining competence across the lifespan (Greene, 2014). Resilient people share "...the ability to tell their stories to an interested and empathic listener in a safe space, especially to someone who has been there and understands" (Konvisser, 2016, p. 17). For those who have suffered trauma, they can integrate painful emotions and make them part of their story to continue living in a productive way (Konvisser, 2016). Stories are evidence of personal meaning (Polkinghorne, 2007), and storytelling enhances the resilience of listeners as well as tellers of stories (East, Jackson, O'Brienn, & Peters, 2010). By reflecting on the personal stories of others, understanding and insight can be gained into "...how others have overcome and worked through their adversity and hardship, and how we can incorporate these insights into our lives and experiences." (East et al., 2010 p. 21).

The earliest roots of *Cruzando Puentes* began with Connie Corley, when she joined a study of Holocaust survivors in California which ended in a culminating public education event at the Los Angeles Museum of the Holocaust called "Holocaust Survivors: Stories of Resilience" featuring the art of three Hungarian survivors, and two members of the study shared their life stories. Later on, the survivors met with university students from CSULA and Fielding to continue reflecting on the devastation in Hungary during World War II and how their art reflected some of these experiences. A model called *Experience, Expression, Engagement (3E)* was formulated (Corley, 2010), leading to a conceptualization of *Cruzando Puentes*, a project in which members of the community of practice share experiences and various forms of aesthetic and academic expression (e.g., academic assignments, poetry readings, visual ethnography). Later on, participants of *Cruzando Puentes* presented the stories to wider audiences who are similarly engaged in community research (e.g., for members of the Society for Applied Anthropology in Philadelphia through a Symposium on Boyle Heights in Spring 2018).

In *communitas*, events bring people together for experiences that include storytelling and other powerful ways of expanding knowledge of adverse life circumstances and how resilience can emerge. The outcome of *communitas*, when stories of resilience are shared, is that resilience of the individuals who have engaged in dialog is fostered. The resilience of the communities in which these members live grows as they are connected to other community members. A sense of the larger whole and sharing common concerns are further reinforced through these experiences.

Reinforcing Resilience in Communities

Community institutions such as universities can contribute to resilience among their members and also to sustaining the institutions at large (Greene & Dubus, 2017). The broader range of resilience of communities, for example the neighborhood/region in which a university is located, is also key. While a predominant focus on resilience in communities has targeted disaster preparation and response as in the Rockefeller Foundation's Resilient Cities initiative (Rockefeller Foundation, 2018) and others (Norris, Stevens, Wyche & Pfefferbaum, 2008), communities in transition, such as Boyle Heights in Los Angeles, can have other triggers for enhanced resilience. These include the provision of visibility of the strengths of the community members and preservation of its history. In *Cruzando Puentes* this examination of what builds resilience was fostered through ethnographic exploration and visual ethnography. Through *communitas*, students and faculty had opportunities to engage with each other while visiting the partner organizations and gain an appreciation of the community context and systems within each of the organizations.

Further Notes on Methods: Visual Ethnography and the Community of Practice

Along with human development as a field of study, which included narrative, ethnography, and history, we employed *visual ethnography*, a unique methodology. Visual ethnography is a sub-field of cultural anthropology that aims to document visual representations of lived experience (Lenette & Boddy, 2013; Pink, 2013). It has roots in anthropology, where disciplinary boundary crossing brings together various theories, practices of art, and photography, with anthropological theory and practice (Pink et al., 2016). Among the reasons for the recent growth in popularity of visual ethnography is that visual ethnographers contend that some cultural elements are best represented visually and pairs with fieldwork very well because this method speaks to representation for both researcher(s) and participants (Pink, 2012, 2013).

We crossed many borders, both physically and metaphorically, during the LA Intensive, but especially in our time in Boyle Heights. We felt it was important to understand the lenses through which our ethnographic observations of the neighbourhood were situated. The lenses were different for each of us. For example, Eliza von Baeyer, stated: "I was a Canadian, studying at Fielding Graduate University in California by distance. I had never been to LA other than transferring flights at LAX, and my family and historical narratives were intertwined with Ellis Island, and not the West Coast immigration of Jews fleeing Nazi Europe."

Students turned to visual ethnography to produce a visual narrative that they shared in a group presentation for their Fielding course once they returned home. Early ethnographers, especially Margaret Mead and Gregory Bateson, were pioneers in using photography to augment their fieldnotes (Holm, 2014; Shembri & Boyle, 2013; Varde, 2005). Bateson and Mead (1942) employed this "new method of stating the intangible relationships among different types of culturally standardized behaviours by placing side by side mutually relevant photographs" (p. xii). Since then, visual ethnography has been becoming increasingly popular for qualitative research, especially in cross-cultural studies, both as a step in the process of data generation and serving as core cultural data itself.

Eliza von Baeyer, David Blake Willis, Wayne Chang, and other members of the LA Intensive (described in Phase Two) took many photographs of Boyle Heights. Eliza then organized the photographs into triptychs as she analyzed the visual and cultural borders we crossed in Boyle Heights and Downtown LA through the lenses of visual ethnography. Eliza's paper was presented at the Symposium in *Society for Applied Anthropology Conference* in April 2018 in Philadelphia, Pennsylvania, with five others, several of whom are mentioned above. Emphasizing visual and social media, she traced Boyle Heights' evolution from a significant immigration hub to its contentious present and a potentially sustainable future.

Boyle Heights: The Challenges of Crossroads Cultures and Stories of Resilience

In rapidly changing communities, diverse groups facing challenges reside together but are often disconnected. Boyle Heights, a well-known neighborhood in Los Angeles is historically significant as an intersection of many cultures and faiths. In more recent decades, the community became a notorious home for gangs (peaking in the 1980s), and presently it is challenged by gentrification. With approximately half of the population under eighteen and nearly all residents being Latino, there are also elders who are immigrants (often first-generation residents of the United States) who live largely disconnected from their neighbors, in several retirement communities. The current population of older adults in Los Angeles County (the second largest metropolitan area in the United States and the largest in California) is over 1.1 million and expected to double by the year 2030. In approximately two decades the three largest ethnic minority groups (Hispanics, Asian/ Pacific Islanders, and African-Americans) will comprise two-thirds of Los Angeles' older adult population (University of Southern California, USC Edward Roybal Institute, 2015).

Currently a resident of the greater LA area, Connie has been involved in lifelong learning programming in one of the retirement communities in Boyle Heights (Hollenbeck Palms) in conjunction with California State University Los Angeles (CSULA) for over 10 years. As a professor emerita from CSULA, Connie established a center for lifelong learning. She saw Hollenbeck Palms residents thrive when sharing their stories and engaging with students who represented different generations and cultures. In Hollenbeck Palms, residents have very little interaction with younger people in the nearby community, many of whom are challenged by gang violence, underemployment, and a landscape now changing due to gentrification. Gentrification, or the displacement of low-income residents (which has transformed several other communities near downtown Los Angeles), is expanding to Boyle Heights.

Like Connie, David is a professor at Fielding Graduate University, and as a cultural anthropologist he has long been interested in marginalized urban communities that are invisible or overlooked. His research began with work in Roxbury, Boston, in the 1960s and in the South Side of Chicago, where he lived in the 1970s. The vibrant creation of community in these two locations has been mirrored by what David has witnessed in his work with Dalits (once pejoratively referred to as 'untouchables') in urban South India, including Dalit drummers and other musicians as well as meat merchants and entrepreneurs. His research focus on migration, diaspora, and transnational communities and is also relevant to the historical shifts currently impacting Boyle Heights and downtown Los Angeles.

Graduate students have also contributed to this community of practice. A doctoral student at Fielding and community activist concerned with organizational systems, Diyana Dobberteen was introduced to Boyle Heights with a cohort of Fielding students during the Los Angeles Intensive Phase Two of *Cruzando Puentes*. Diyana's inquiry revealed that gentrification in Boyle Heights stems from macro-system changes and she studied resilience in terms of how Boyle Heights' community activists are responding to gentrification's impacts. Student colleague and co-author, Eliza von Baeyer, a Canadian from Ottawa, was drawn to the politically infused art she saw represented in public murals in Boyle Heights as evidence of community resilience and a strong cultural identity, both past and present. A brief description of visual ethnography as a method, as well as insights that Eliza gained along with fellow students are presented in our discussion of Phase Two.

The Story of *Cruzando Puentes*: Project Phases and Community Partners

Designed as an exploratory case study (Yin, 2003b, in Berg, 2009) *Cruzando Puentes* started as a Social Transformation Project and continued as an ongoing collaborative research endeavor with the goal of creating a model for intergenerational and intercultural engagement that could be adapted for other communities of practice. The research question guiding the case study was "*How can a community of practice integrate academic and service settings to promote intergenerational*

211

and intercultural mentoring?" The project data includes written and visual narratives, value narratives, and reports of a range of activities by partners in the project team.

As a participatory, multi-phased research project, we were also interested in exploring the possibility that the resilience capacity of this community of practice may be enhanced through the narrative element. More than just gathering data for analysis, this critical dimension of the project included storytelling among members of the community and visual narratives of the people and spaces in the community. In each of three separate project phases, stories of resilience were gathered. Several photos illustrate a visual ethnographic component of *Cruzando Puentes*.

Summarizing the Three Project Phases

Phase One of *Cruzando Puentes* involved defining the community of practice, establishing the networks, intersecting and interacting with the communities, and collecting narratives. Phase Two engaged students in a community of practice, an ethnographic/human development practicum that was a three-day intensive educational and social change experience. Phase Three was a research project examining mutual mentoring over meals at the Homegirl Café at Homeboy Industries, bringing together three teams of older adults/former gang members for three meals.

Partners in The Case Study

Fielding Graduate University. Essential to the mission and vision of its founders in 1974, our university's approach to learning involves enhancing the capacities of the already accomplished adult learners to grow as scholars who put their knowledge into practice for the greater good. The learning model of Fielding Graduate University (Fielding) is designed to be supportive, self-directed, global, and rigorous. In 2015 Fielding was awarded the Carnegie Community Engagement classification due to its commitment as a publicly engaged university (Melville, 2016). The *Institute for Social Innovation* at Fielding Graduate University supports this Social Transformation Project and other initiatives to build human capital and sustainable change. Most students are working professionals, and in the *Cruzando Puentes* community of practice the participating students were enrolled in doctoral degree programs in Human Development as well as Organizational Development and Change.

California State University Los Angeles. California State University Los Angeles (CSULA) was founded in 1947 and enrolls over 20,000 students annually. It is one of the 23 campuses in the California State University system and a designated Hispanic-Serving Institution. In 2014 President William Covino launched The Center for Engagement, Service, and the Public Good in order to create a hub of civic engagement and public service for the city of Los Angeles and its communities and region. Service learning and neighborhood transformation are seen as a catalytic force for students, faculty and community residents. Our key CSULA partner throughout was Siouxsie Calderón, MSW, an alumna of the CSULA School of Social Work and adjunct faculty.

Hollenbeck Palms Retirement Community. Located in the Boyle Heights area of Los Angeles, Hollenbeck Palms was established in 1890 as Hollenbeck Home and was the first licensed retirement community in the state of California. It is independently owned and operated as a nonprofit organization (www.hollenbeckpalms.org). Living arrangements support those who live independently, as well as residents in need of assisted living and skilled nursing. Most residents are over 80 years of age and many are immigrants or are the first-generation born in the United States, including Japanese Americans who had lived in the area decades ago. Many of the Japanese Americans who had lived in this community were disenfranchised and displaced during the World War II due to their internment.

Homeboy Industries. Homeboy Industries (www.homeboyindustries.org) is the largest gang-intervention project in the United States, founded by Fr. Gregory Boyle in 1992. Fr. Boyle is well known for his book *Tattoos on the Heart* (Boyle, 2010) and more recently for the follow up book, *Barking to the Choir* (2017). Originating in Boyle Heights, Homeboy's headquarters is now located in the Chinatown area of downtown Los Angeles. Thousands of formerly gang-involved men and women are offered supportive services (e.g., case management, mental health services, tattoo removal) and job-training through Homeboy. A thriving nonprofit organization, Homeboy operates social enterprises and provides on-site training for a variety of jobs in food service, recycling, electronic remanufacture, and teaches teamwork, and other skills. "Nothing Stops a Bullet Like a Job" is a motto on t-shirts made and sold by Homeboy.

Phase One: Original Project Plan and Case Study

The fall of 2015 marked the launch of *Cruzando Puentes* when project directors Connie Corley and David Blake Willis organized a team of faculty, students, and alumni from Fielding Graduate University to meet with older adults at Hollenbeck Palms Retirement Community. The team then explored prospects for engaging California State University Los Angeles through on-site programs like the Mobility Center at CSULA, which provides direct engagement of students with older adults on campus.

The *Cruzando Puentes* project team also spent time at Homeboy Industries and engaged in ethnographic observation in the Mariachi Plaza neighborhood in Boyle Heights, the East LA center of Latinx and Chicanx Culture, visiting colorful and unique stores nearby and outdoor vendors in the evening. Field visits gave the research team a sense of the richness of this vibrant community, which is rapidly changing. New businesses are entering the area and some of the character of the largely Latinx community is showing signs of displacement by gentrification and what some locals have called art-washing, or the increase in retail art galleries in this low-income community. Locals feel that business ventures and nonprofits cater mostly to rich, Caucasian non-residents.

View of Mariachi Plaza in Boyle Heights, Los Angeles
in the background.

In spring 2016 students in two social work courses taught by CSULA adjunct Siouxsie Calderón, "Social Policy and Aging" plus "Cross Cultural Practice with Older Adults," had opportunities for direct interaction with older adults. Students in the policy class along with nutritional science students met with participants on campus who come to the Mobility Center, which provides students in kinesiology direct practice experiences with persons who have had strokes and other challenges impacting their mobility. Ms. Calderón also added a field trip component to the course, *Cross Cultural Practice with Older Adults*. One site was Hollenbeck Palms, where Connie provided a tour and invited a 90-year old resident who was a former activities director there and other residents to share about life at Hollenbeck. Members of the study team and a student from CSULA followed up with interviews of residents who had been met on the Hollenbeck Palms campus.

Phase One: A Story of Resilience

Erika C., student from CSULA, interviewed a 95-year-old Holocaust survivor living at Hollenback Palms (Erica L.), returning to meet with her after the class of students went for a site visit. Although Erika C. is from a different cultural background and generation than Erica L., who immigrated to the U.S. at age 70, their engagement with each other demonstrated immediate value for Erika C., plus potential value and applied value for her career aspirations. The experience of mutual mentoring enhanced each woman's sense of resilience as each was affirmed in the context of the relationship. Here are quotes from Erika C.'s paper for the "Cross-Cultural Practice and Older Adults" class:

> My feelings about aging began to stir up after witnessing my *abuelita* [Spanish for 'grandmother'] endure a painful and life ending experience. Having had the opportunity to visit with Erica L. only puts life into perspective. Toward the end of our visit she requested I wheel her to the garden, and we sat listening to the chirping birds while admiring the roses after a day of rain. To document Erica L's story and apply it to my life is a treat since I can understand life better today. I don't understand why individuals go through horrific life changing situations, but I know that I have the power to be an advocate to individuals like my *abuelita* and Erica L. By expressing her experience, strength, and hope to others, we can learn from her tenacity so that others can be influenced. She continues to inspire others with her creative artistic creations and with her testimony."
> (Erika C., personal communication, June 2016)

Phase Two: An Educational Intensive

As an extension of the model incorporating *communitas* we then planned Phase Two, "The Los Angeles Intensive", which began with a multi-day educational program tied into the academic work of Fielding doctoral students in January 2017. Ethnographic observations of the Boyle Heights community including Hollenbeck Palms were part of the Intensive, as well as a tour and meal at the headquarters of Homeboy Industries. Opportunities to hear stories of older adults as well as former gang members were built into the experience. Participants included eleven Fielding doctoral students and faculty, Siouxsie Calderón and students from CSULA, along with residents of Hollenbeck Palms and Homeboy staff. Daily debriefings took place in order to process observations, field notes, and direct engagement with each other and community sites.

We often met over meals. These included a dinner with the older residents of Hollenbeck following the screening of Kalin's documentary on Boyle Heights, *East LA Interchange (See: http://www. eastlainterchangefilm.com),* and lunch at the Homegirl Café after an extensive tour of Homeboy's headquarters. These scheduled events and other spontaneous opportunities (including a poetry reading by Mike Sonksen, LA native, journalist, and advocate for LA communities) provided rich opportunities for teams of students to work together in *communitas*.

Several weeks following the LA Intensive, students presented the perspectives and lessons learned to a larger whole group that had engaged in an online platform for an academic term and course credit. Further, some students presented their insights and analyses from the LA Intensive at the *Society for Applied Anthropology Conference* in Philadelphia, Pennsylvania, United States, in April 2018.

Phase Two LA Intensive: Making a Connection
at Hollenbeck Palms

Phase Two: Stories of Resilience

During the Intensive, our team had an opportunity to dine with residents at Hollenbeck Palms and also take an extended tour of Homeboy Industries, which included lunch at the Homegirl Café. Students shared how experiencing deeply personal storytelling changed their perspectives and expanded their understanding of the role of resilience.

> *Cruzando Puentes* took me to places I would not
> have gone to on my own. We ate dinner with intern-
> ment camps survivors (WWII) who went into depth
> about the trials they faced with their families and
> overcame. It was profound, and I now appreciate how
> resilience impacts a lifecourse. (Diyana Dobberteen,
> personal communication, February 2018)

Another Fielding student, Wayne Chang, wrote a paper following the LA Intensive examining the relationship between forgiveness and resilience entitled, "Forgiveness, resilience and attributes of posttraumatic growth" (Chang, 2017) in which he noted:

218

An example of someone attributing forgiveness to bouncing back is "Danny," a former gang member... at Homeboy Industries.... He described his forgiveness in accepting his wife back after a hiatus in his marriage: "However, when she returned to my side, I, uh, I had a choice to make. I could either harbor the resentment of her abandonment of our marriage, and the love that we had held, or I could forgive. And I had stumbled across this adage that says, 'in order to live, you must forgive.' And for me there is only one choice, because I missed everything about it. So, I welcomed her back in to my life and my heart."

Danny also welcomed a son, at the time nearly three years old, that his wife had during their time apart. Because he forgave his wife and allowed both her and her new son back into his life, he noted that, "I am still the only guy that [his son] knows his dad to be. And I'm grateful that I made that choice because it gave me a greater sense of purpose in life." He sees forgiveness as protecting him from hardships: "There's a wonderful understanding that, you know, in life we often can injure those that are dearest to our heart. So, I think forgiveness is inherent in life because that puts a blanket of love over whatever it is that sometimes pops up." (Danny, 2017 in Chang, 2017)

In these brief but impactful encounters our sense of *communitas* inspired a plan for research that included prolonged engagements and led to Phase Three of *Cruzando Puentes*.

Phase Three: Research at Homeboy Industries

Cruzando Puentes evolved into a pilot project in Phase Three, engaging students and alumni from Fielding Graduate University in observing and interviewing teams of older adults and Homeboys/ Homegirls as they met multiple times over meals at the Homegirl Café in downtown LA in Summer, 2017. Preliminary analysis of the "meals and mentoring" research suggests that by talking over meals, sharing life experiences, and learning about one another, people can transcend differences and appreciate commonalities. Social isolation is reduced, intergenerational as well as intercultural interchange is fostered, and resilience is enhanced through mutual affirmation of experiences of thriving after adversity.

We met our goal of creating bridges across generations and cultures to foster mutual mentoring and contribute to the resilience of the participants in a series of structured engagements and through *communitas*. Interviews with the participants after the series of meals revealed the following themes: life course lessons, cultural connections, and comfort in sharing. Among comments from the Homeboy participants was their surprise at commonalities in some life experiences, appreciation for differences, and being able to talk about them openly. Deep connections formed for some dyads, and each valued having meaningful exchanges with people, whom they would not normally meet, in a safe environment out of the range of daily experiences.

Phase Three: Stories of Resilience

In one of the teams, two men who grew up in Boyle Heights in different eras (the 1950s–1960s compared to the 1980s–1990s) happened to have other unexpected commonalities – both having a paralyzed arm and both having served time in jail. Over three meals they learned why each had moved away from Boyle Heights and shared the experiences that led to their current lives. The younger man said of his elder companion, "His story was, I thought it was pretty crazy. Because of all the luck that he mentioned – I am sure that it wasn't all luck." His statement implies the elder member demonstrated resilience given all he had endured (such as challenges with addiction, loss of marriage, a health problem resulting in paralysis). Both men talked about the "luck" each of them had experienced surviving various life challenges, but their resilience in the face of violence, injuries (the gang member had been paralyzed by a gunshot), and jail time was not just a matter of chance. Their mutual trust and the instant connection they had was remarkable.

Homegirl Café – A Site for Meals and Mentoring in Los Angeles

Another of the Homeboy teams, in this case two women, bonded over their three meals together. The 'Homegirl' was in the early part of her 18-month engagement in the Homeboy program and was recruited for *Cruzando Puentes* to give her an opportunity to share her story one-to-one in preparation for a later commitment to share her story with groups of people on tours. She noted that it was hard to talk about the story of how she got to Homeboy following incarceration, but that more intimate sharing over meals allowed her to 'open up" and recognize commonalities with an older woman she would not have known outside of *Cruzando Puentes*. The experience gave her new perspectives on how people can connect across age and cultural differences. She has since been hired by a local agency after completing the Homeboy program.

Cruzando Puentes and Resilience

Cruzando Puentes offered a new lens on generations and cultures through visual and oral narratives. It built the resilience of members within a community in transition due to gentrification, and it empowered vulnerable young adults (former gang members), students, and elders (including survivors of the Holocaust, the World War II Japanese internment camps, and other challenging experiences) through mutual mentoring and opportunities to share lessons from the lifecourse.

In each phase, stories of resilience were shared in planned engagements across members of the community of practice partner organizations. These experiences of *communitas* provided more in-depth engagement than the more typical visits to an organization; for example, going beyond a typical Homeboy Industries tour, by sharing meals together in Phase Three. The process allowed younger and older adults to go deeper in conversation. Also, through subsequent engagements with Homeboy that occurred throughout the phases, Connie found application for her experience/expression/engagement model in multiple interactions. What worked well with Holocaust survivors was transferable to other populations (in this case former gang members). Sharing meals and learning from elders who have survived life-threatening situations built the former gang members' capacity to share stories of personal resilience more widely. Eventually, this Fielding study resulted in engaging with a larger public, through academic presentations and publications about *Cruzando Puentes*, our means of representing the essence of "radical kinship" which Homeboy founder Fr. Gregory Boyle describes in *Barking to the Choir* (2017).

Similar to lessons from her work with Holocaust survivors, Connie met her goal of providing a wider lens on the lifecourse experiences of people who embody resilience. Communities of LA and elsewhere are well-served when students/alumni/faculty from universities engage with members of communities and become connected to community settings through *communitas*. The resilience of the individuals as well as the communities they represent is enhanced, as noted by Siouxsie from CSULA (Corley & Willis, 2016).

> My participation in *Cruzando Puentes* has opened up a new way and style to my overall teaching philosophy. My confidence and connection to the campus, local life, and East Los Angeles has expanded more than expected. I am known as an expert in the field of aging and housing, and… feel competent in being able to take a group of students on field trips to where our elders live, play, and convalesce…I get to influence future social workers on why, where, and how to work with our elders. [In] student evaluations [some] state they have changed their major after taking the class with the field trips out to East LA senior sites. The School of Social Work has also recognized the field trips through sharing pictures and stories about our field trips out in the community. (Siouxsie Calderón, personal communication, June 2016)

Coming Full Circle: Boyle Heights as Resilient Community

As our principal partners in this collaborative and creative partnership between generations, the people of Boyle Heights prominently included elders with a long-term stake in the community from many different cultural perspectives. The award-winning historical documentary film previously noted, *East LA Interchange,* poignantly demonstrates this – how Boyle Heights has had many communities of practice. The Boyle Heights community breaks the conventional definition of community and is a powerful case study in many senses of the word. Like similar urban neighborhoods around the world, Boyle Heights provides a vibrant and lively tapestry which needs to be reported and made visible. The invisibility, indeed, has been a major disruptive force in the lives of many in the Los Angeles area, as the battles around Chavez Ravine and elsewhere show quite powerfully. Similarly, the yearnings and struggles of diasporic communities commemorate historical memory, power, and resistance that have cultural identity at the core of the changes that we witness over time – reflections of ethnicity, race, and gender in particular eras.

Boyle Heights locals' impressions of the changing character of this modern hub of Chicanx culture were of interest to Fielding student, Diyana. Through reading about this issue in media, online, and via informal interviews she learned that rising rents, retail displacement, the introduction of art galleries, and real estate speculation threaten the community. Changes accelerated after 2009, when the LA Metro Gold Line linked Boyle Heights to downtown Los Angeles. The Gold Line, the name given to the Metro Line running through Boyle Heights, is symbolic of this. The rapid connection to the core it has initiated created a community-wide shift. As noted in a 2015 UCLA study of gentrification and transit in Los Angeles, construction of new transit often paves the way for gentrification (UCLA, 2015)

Residents of Boyle Heights who are threatened by recent socio-economic changes are resisting. Predominantly Chicanx/ Latinx community members (immigrants, low-income residents and young adults) step into roles as activists opposing new threats to their livelihoods. They are organizing for cultural survival, rent control, greater community participation, and changes to community development policy (Almazan, 2017). As in other United States urban centers, growth and macro-political systems continue to challenge the resilience of Boyle Heights residents.

Conclusion

We have presented the components of a Social Transformation Project launched from seed funding and research support from one university, in collaboration with community partners and intersecting two universities that focused on the historic and richly diverse Boyle Heights neighborhood of Los Angeles and adjacent downtown Los Angeles. Situating the project as a community of practice, engaging members in *communitas*, and examining the use of ethnographic and narrative approaches has enabled us to locate points of tension and transformation as well as meeting places of harmony and social growth.

In the three phases of this project, both the open exchange of personal stories and the perspectives that participants gained in hearing about resilience over the lifecourse, were a result of *communitas*. As Los Angeles and Boyle Heights continue to grapple with complex realities of urban policy-making, an aging population, changing community demographics and modern cultural hybridity, advocates may consider this Fielding/CSULA/nonprofit organization community of practice as a model. Among areas for future research and visual ethnography are defining the avenues for community participation, expanding options for developing a space for cultural exchanges, and initiating projects that are intergenerational.

In conclusion, a surprising outcome of *Cruzando Puentes* is the resilience of our larger community of practice and the community itself. Four years plus after its inception, several individuals linked to our community, who took part in building this Social Transformation Project are still connected to the Boyle Heights community and other Los Angeles organizations that we engaged.

Acknowledgements

The authors wish to acknowledge the support from the Fielding Graduate University Institute for Social Innovation and the faculty, students, and alumni who engaged in *Cruzando Puentes*. Hollenbeck Palms staff and residents, Homeboy staff and interns, and California State University Los Angeles students and faculty have been instrumental in the success of this community of practice. Parts of this manuscript are included in Corley and Willis (2016), reprinted with permission. Photos were taken by Connie Corley, David Blake Willis, and Eliza von Baeyer.

References

Almazan, S. (September 17, 2017). Gente de Boyle Heights: Rise and stand for your community! *Berkeley Public Policy Journal,* originally in *Boyle Heights Beat*, retrieved from: https://bppj. berkeley.edu/2017/09/19/perspective-gente-de-boyle-heights-rise-and-stand-for-your-community/

Bateson, G., & Mead, M. (1942). *Balinese character: A photographic analysis.* New York, NY: New York Academy of Sciences.

Berg, B. L. (2009). *Qualitative research methods for the social sciences* (7th ed.). Boston, MA: Allyn & Bacon.

Boyle, G. (2010). *Tattoos on the heart: The power of boundless compassion.* New York, NY: Free Press.

Boyle, G. (2017). *Barking to the choir: The power of radical kinship.* New York, NY: Simon & Schuster.

Chang, W. (2017). *Forgiveness, resilience and attributes of posttraumatic growth.* Unpublished manuscript. (Interview at Homeboy Industries, Danny, Los Angeles, California)

Corley, C. (2010). A tale of three women: Survivorship through creative expression. *Journal of Aging, Humanities and the Arts, 4*, 262-275.

Corley, C., & Willis, D. B. (2017). Cruzando Puentes: A social transformation case study. In G. D. Sardana & T. Thatchenkery (Eds.), *Knowledge creation and organizational well-being: Leveraging talent management and appreciative intelligence.* New Delhi, India: Bloomsbury.

East, L., Jackson, D., O'Brien, L., and Peters, K. (2010). Storytelling:

An approach that can help to develop resilience, *Nurse Researcher, 17*(3), 17-25.

Greene, R. (2014). Resilience as effective functional capacity: An ecological-stress model. *Journal of Human Behavior in the Social Environment, 24*, 937–950. doi:10.1080/10911359.2014.921589

Greene, R., & Dubus, N. (2017). *Resilience in action: An information and practice guide.* Washington, DC: NASW Press.

Holm, G. (2014). Photography as research method. In P. Leavy (Ed.), *The Oxford Handbook of Qualitative Research,*1-37. doi:10.1093/oxfordhb/9780199811755.013.031

Kalin, B. (2016). *East LA Interchange.* Documentary film:www.eastlainterchangefilm.com/

Konvisser, Z. (2016). Healing returning veterans: The role of storytelling and community. *Fielding Monograph, 8*, 14-46.

Lenette, C., & Boddy, J. (2013). Visual ethnography and refugee women: Nuanced understandings of lived experience. *Qualitative Research Journal, 13(1),* 72-89. doi:10.1108/14439881311314621

Melville, K. (2016). *A passion for adult learning: How the Fielding model is transforming doctoral education.* Santa Barbara, CA: Fielding University Press.

Napier, G. (2016). *Beyond Community: Understanding the Experience of Communitas Among Information Technology Road Warriors.* (Doctoral dissertation). Retrieved from https://fgul.idm.oclc.org/docview/1858815110?accountid=10868

Norris, F. H., Stevens, S. P., Wyche, K. F., & Pfefferbaum, R. L. (2008). Community resilience as a metaphor, theory, set of capacities, and strategy for disaster readiness. *American Journal of Community Psychology, 41*, 127–150.

Pink, S. (2012). *Advances in visual methodology.* Thousand Oaks, CA: Sage Publications.

Pink, S. (2013). *Doing visual ethnography* (3rd ed.). Thousand Oaks,

CA: Sage Publications.

Pink, S., Horst, H., Postill, J., Hjorth, L., Lewis, T., & Tacchi, J. (2016). *Digital ethnography: Principles and practice.* Thousand Oaks, CA: Sage Publications.

Polkinghorne, D. E. (2007). Validity issues in narrative research. *Qualitative Inquiry 13*(4), 471-486. doi:10.1177/1077800406297670

Rockefeller Foundation (2018). *Resilient Cities - 100 Resilient Cities Report*, Retrieved from: https://www.rockefellerfoundation. org/report/city-resilience-index-2/

Shembri, S., & Boyle, M. V. (2013). Visual ethnography: Achieving rigorous and authentic interpretations. *Journal of Business Research (66),* 1251-1254. doi:10.1016/j.jbusres.2012.02.021

Turner, E. (2012). *Communitas: The anthropology of collective joy.* New York, NY: Palgrave Macmillan. https://doi. org/10.1057/9781137016423_1

Turner, V. (1974). *Dramas, fields, and metaphors: Symbolic action in human society.* Cornell, NY: Cornell University Press.

University of California, Los Angeles (UCLA) (2015). *The 2015 Comprehensive Project Report- Oriented for Whom? The Impacts of TOD on Six Los Angeles Neighborhoods* (Unpublished Master's thesis) Retrieved from: http://www.urbandisplacement. org/sites/default/files/images/spring_2015_tod.pdf, Los Angeles, California.

University of Southern California (USC) Edward Roybal Institute on Aging (2015). *The 2015 Los Angeles Healthy Aging Report.* Retrieved from:http://roybal.usc.edu/wp-content/uploads/2016/04/USC_Roybal-LA_HealthyAging.pdf

Varde, A. (2005*). Local looking, developing a context-specific model for visual ethnography: A representational study of child labor in India.* (Doctoral dissertation). Retrieved from http://rave. ohiolink.edu/etdc/view?acc_num=osu1132682652

Wenger, E. (2000). Communities of practice and social learning organizations. *Organization,* 7(2), 225-246.

Wenger, E., McDermott, R., & Snyder, W. M. (2002). *Cultivating communities of practice: A guide to managing knowledge.* Boston, MA: HBR Press.

About the Authors

Connie Corley, PhD has a long history of engagement in the fields of gerontology and geriatrics since her graduate studies at the University of Michigan, Ann Arbor beginning in the late 1970s. As a doctoral faculty member in the School of Leadership Studies at Fielding Graduate University, Dr. Corley leads the doctoral concentration in Creative Longevity and Wisdom. She is Professor Emeritus at California State University, Los Angeles. A Fellow of the Gerontological Society of America and the Academy of Gerontology in Higher Education, Dr. Corley has earned numerous awards of distinction. She has been engaged in multiple programs as a mentor and leader in curriculum development. Her work has involved creativity in later life (emerging out of a national study of Holocaust survivors, led by Roberta Greene, PI). She created the "Experience, Engagement, Expression" model, demonstrating successive levels of engagement and wider ranging expression of creativity based on life experiences. The model inspired the multi-year *Cruzando Puentes* ("Crossing Bridges"), an intergenerational and intercultural community of practice in diverse communities of Los Angeles. Dr. Corley co-hosts and produces a radio show on KPFK-FM in Los Angeles (Experience Talks), interviewing guests who are seasoned in life. Dr. Corley may be contacted at ccorley@fielding.edu.

David Blake Willis, PhD is Professor of Anthropology and Education at Fielding Graduate University and Professor Emeritus of Anthropology at Soai Buddhist University in Osaka, Japan. He taught and did research at the University of Oxford and has been Visiting Professor at Grinnell College and the University of Washington. His interests in anthropology, community, social justice, sustainability, and immigration come from nearly 40 years living in traditional cultural systems in Japan and India. He researches and writes on transformational community, leadership and education, human development in transnational contexts, the Creolization of cultures, transcultural communities, and Dalit/Gandhian liberation movements in South India. His publications include *World Cultures – The Language Villages* with Walter Enloe; *Sustainability Leadership: Integrating Values, Meaning, and Action* with Fred Steier and Paul Stillman (2015); *Reimagining Japanese Education: Borders, Transfers, Circulations, and the Comparative* with Jeremy Rappleye (2011); *Transcultural Japan: At the Borders of Race, Gender, and Identity* with Stephen Murphy-Shigematsu (2007); and *Japanese Education in Transition 2001: Radical Perspectives on Cultural and Political Transformation* with Satoshi Yamamura (2002). Dr. Willis may be contacted at dwillis@fielding.edu.

Diyana Dobberteen, MA is pursuing a doctoral degree at Fielding Graduate University. Previously she earned a Master's Degree in ethnography from University of California, Santa Barbara (UCSD) and a Bachelor's Degree in anthropology from University of California, San Diego (UCSB). Her dissertation research addresses organizational learning within the global climate justice movement. She will apply social movement theory and organizational learning theory to better understand how issue frames diffuse across interorganizational coalitions as they engage in climate action online. Diyana has a depth of capacity building, community outreach, and program development experience having implemented numerous programs: teenage pregnancy prevention strategies, college access for underrepresented students, and public health education. In a nonprofit consulting role, she worked with Fielding's President, Katrina Rogers, Ph.D., and faculty to bring affordable consulting to nonprofit organizations in the Santa Barbara community (2006-2007). A child welfare agency and alcohol rehabilitation nonprofit were among the clients. She recalls how data-driven solutions from Fielding's strategic planning with participating organizations significantly improved services and in turn increased community resilience. In addition, Diyana helped Fielding's *Worldwide Network for Gender Empowerment* to partner with the local Planned Parenthood affiliate and conduct a regional LGB&T sexual health community needs assessment (2016-2017). Diyana may be contacted at ddobberteen@email.fielding.edu.

Eliza von Baeyer, MA is currently a PhD student in the Organizational Development and Change program at Fielding Graduate University and a graduate of its year-long certificate in evidence-based coaching. Over her time at Fielding, arts-based research and ethnography have become central to her coursework and the development of her dissertation. They are natural extensions of her life-long artistic endeavours, such as photography, jewelry making and collage work; activities that have previously taken a back seat to her academic and employment activities. During the same time period as her coursework, she helped resettle Tibetan refugees in Ottawa, Canada, which along with arts-based methods, informs her dissertation. She is combining visual ethnographic and photovoice methods to study the resettlement of Tibetan women, skills she also applied to the intensive in Boyle Heights, discussed in this monograph. When not working on a Fielding-related academic activity, she can be found in Ottawa working as an organizational psychologist specializing in change management, coaching, and program evaluation, using the scholar-practitioner model as the foundation to her work, and including the arts wherever she can. Eliza may be contacted at evonbaeyer@email.fielding.edu.

About the Editors

Marie Sonnet, PhD (Co-Editor) worked in quality and process improvement initiatives across multiple industries utilizing improvement science methodologies like Six Sigma, Toyota Production Systems, and Professional Project Management. While an internal consultant in a healthcare organization, Dr. Sonnet began to incorporate behavior science with improvement science as way to address the critical, but often underrecognized, people side of planned change initiatives. As the rate of change increased, both planned and unplanned, she noted that needed capabilities for responding to change and adversity were hard if not impossible to create in the moment. A systematic approach was needed to build a ready and reliable storehouse of change capabilities. As a practitioner scholar, she found that building organizational resilience capacity as a strategic resource, built up as employees worked together could result in a readiness strategy that was specific, measurable, and accountable. Following the lead of other scholars, Dr. Sonnet sought to find out which beliefs and behaviors a change ready and capable organization would deliberately foster and support.

Dr. Sonnet continues her research and practice as a Fielding Graduate University Institute for Social Innovation Fellow and is Owner and Principal at Sonnet Organization Consulting. Dr. Sonnet may be reached at msonnet@email.fielding.edu or by visiting her website at www.mariesonnet.com.

Connie Corley, PhD (Co-Editor) is a Professor at Fielding Graduate University in the School of Leadership Studies, Professor Emeritus at California State University, Los Angeles and adjunct faculty member at Saybrook University. In graduate school at the University of Michigan, Ann Arbor, she learned about the field of gerontology and has largely worked in this arena for over four decades. Dr. Corley has presented internationally and published on multiple aspects of positive aging, including creativity, spirituality, resilience, and intergenerational and intercultural engagement.

A Fellow of the Gerontological Society of America and the Academy for Gerontology in Higher Education, Dr. Corley has also been a mentor in the New Ventures in Leadership program of the American Society on Aging. In administrative roles, she has had oversight of research and training programs at Duke University Medical Center as well as California State University, Los Angeles, and was involved in multiple Hartford Geriatric Social Work initiatives including mentoring and curriculum development roles. Active in the Association for Gerontology in Social Work Education (AGESW) as a Past President and former Board member, Dr. Corley is a recipient of the Leadership Award from AGESW. In 2004, she was the inaugural recipient of the West Coast Gerontological Social Work Career Award from the Institute for Geriatric Social Work. California State University, Los Angeles named Dr. Corley a Distinguished Woman in 2008.

Dr. Corley co-hosts and produces a radio program at Pacifica station KPFK-FM in Los Angeles (Experience Talks), interviewing guests who are seasoned in life. She may be contacted at ccorley@ fielding.edu.

About Fielding Graduate University

Fielding Graduate University, headquartered in Santa Barbara, CA, was founded in 1974 and celebrates its 45th anniversary in 2019. Fielding is an accredited, nonprofit leader in blended graduate education, combining face-to-face and online learning. Its curriculum offers quality master's and doctoral degrees for professionals and academics around the world. Fielding's faculty members represent a wide spectrum of scholarship and practice in the fields of educational leadership, human and organizational development, and clinical and media psychology. Fielding's faculty serves as mentors and guides to self-directed students who use their skills and professional experience to become powerful, socially responsible leaders in their communities, workplaces, and society. For more information, please visit Fielding online at www.fielding.edu.

About Fielding Graduate University's Institute
for Social Innovation

Social innovation is a novel solution to a problem that is more effective, sustainable, or just than current approaches. Since 2002, Fielding's Institute for Social Innovation (ISI) has helped individuals as well as nonprofit, business, and government organizations address societal problems via research, professional development, and organizational consulting. ISI professionals include Fielding alumni, faculty, and students who conduct action-oriented research, train organizational leaders, lead community dialogues, and provide customized organizational consulting. Through the Institute for Social Innovation, Fielding earned the Carnegie Foundation Community Engagement Classification in 2010 and 2015. Research and social change projects demonstrated community impact and a strong relationship to student learning. For more information, please visit the ISI online at www.fielding.edu/our-programs/institute-for-social-innovation/.